Following God Together

LET'S TALK ABOUT FRIENDSHIP

by April Chapman, Julie Davis, & Maureen Knotts

Italics in Scripture quotations have been added by the author for emphasis.

Library of Congress Control Number: 2021907197

ISBN: 978-1-7327854-1-0
Published by Abundant Joy Publishing
Jacksonville, Florida

Contents

Dedication

To every woman desiring deeper friendships,
may God richly bless you.

And to Francine Marshall for speaking over us
all those years ago…and for everything since.

Introduction

by April Chapman

Friendships can begin in unexpected ways. When I was a young mother, living in a new city, I didn't realize I was about to meet two women who would forever be imprinted on my heart and life. Maureen lived only a few doors down from me and within minutes of meeting, we discovered we both had a heart for ministry and it was no accident God had planted us next to each other.

Within days, we planned an outing at our local swimming pool. Since it was Florida and afternoon thunderstorms are a regular occurrence in the summer, it wasn't a surprise when we heard thunder and the lifeguard whistle blow. Closed. We decided to head to my house and wait out the storm, but neither of us knew a divine appointment was just taking shape.

On our walk out, we saw another mom's shattered hopes of a few hours of fun at the pool with her sons. After hearing Julie's sweet Mississippi accent, I invited her to take refuge in my not-so-clean house around the corner, she said yes to a stranger, and our friendship began. The three of us have been the best of friends for over fifteen years now.

Every relationship has the power to teach you. Some friendships will stand the test of time. You will learn things like how to trust, laugh when you feel like crying, and have someone know how you feel after just one word. Then there are bonds that end unexpectedly, or after a disagreement, and these are able to teach you about how to approach your next friendships with more wisdom.

We believe friendships are a blessing and that God desires us to be in community with each other. Join us as we dive into the deep end of how to build meaningful friendships.

Our hearts are for women to have deep friendships with each other and God. In this study, we will look at relationships in the Bible and what they teach us about friendship. And, because we know that your own experience is immensely valuable…we will take time to share and learn from each other using our Friendship Builder questions.

This study encompasses 7 sessions, which includes one introductory week and 6 weeks of homework. We understand that sometimes 5 days of Bible study homework can feel overwhelming, so we settled on **3 days a week**. Enough time to dig into the Word, but not so much that you are cramming in multiple days of homework right before heading out to your group. Yes…we've all been there!

We encourage you to carve out the time to study and reap the rewards of your time investment. However, we know how busy life can be, so if you aren't able to get to it, we have a strict **#NoShame policy**. Please still attend your study group and invest in the friendships you are building! You are a vital part of your group!

Although this study can be done on your own, we encourage you to participate in a group when available, or even just invite a friend or two to join you! Our Leader Guide can be found on page 129.

We have 15-20 minute downloadable **videos** that correlate with your study for the week. Expect to laugh and learn with us as we share how God has used our experiences to create lasting and deep friendships. Find the videos at www.EntwinedMinistries.com.

We are excited you are joining us on this journey! We are praying for you to encounter God and build deeper relationships along the way!

Quick Tip: Although we reference many versions of the Bible, unless otherwise stated, we use the NLT version. You may find it easier in the "fill in the blanks" areas if you look up verses in that version.

About The Authors

April Chapman is an author, speaker, and host of the Audacious Hope podcast. She is passionate about encouraging women in their faith, especially when life doesn't turn out the way they expected. She is a single mom to three daughters, who keep her young, but never tire of reminding her she is still "old." April loves to study the Bible, especially the Old Testament stories, and can easily get lost in those paper-thin magnificent pages.

Julie Davis is a licensed pastor serving kids, families, and women. She was first called to ministry in 2005 when she had little to no idea what that actually meant. But God is good and patient, and she's been learning through little steps of faith ever since. Julie has been married to a great guy for 24 years and has three children. She loves to visit new places, learn new things about God, and watch home improvement shows until her family cries, "No more, Mom!"

Maureen Knotts has served in ministry for over 20 years and is currently the Children's Director at River Christian Church in Fleming Island, Florida. She has been married for 22 years and is the mother of three, including a set of twins now in college. Maureen is passionate about Jesus, children and investing in relationships. She loves to plan events and has a serious case of FOMO (Fear of Missing Out), so fun is always on the agenda!

Introduction Video Notes:

Friendship Builder Questions

Do NOT feel the need to go in order or fit all the questions into the time allotted. Each woman should choose at least one of the questions to ask in her small group. Then get to talking and sharing your hearts with each other!

1. What's your all-time favorite book?
2. What is the most important quality trait you look for in a friend?
3. What brings you joy?
4. When you are venting to someone do you want their advice or to just listen?
5. Are you more likely to undershare or overshare?
6. Would you rather go with a friend to a movie, out to eat, or to a concert?
7. What keeps you up at night?
8. What are some of your hobbies?
9. What is your must-have beauty product?
10. If you were to start a blog, what would it be about?
11. What's your favorite dessert?
12. What TV show do you turn on when you just want to zone out and feel better?

Prayer Requests:

Week One

THE FOUR FRIENDS

This is my favorite Bible story! Well…I have lots of favorites, but this one is at the top of my list. It's got drama, antagonists, a miracle, a crowd of witnesses, and Jesus standing up to powerful naysayers. But this is not just a story. It's a true account of an actual time with actual people. This story was written 2000 years ago to teach us something. Many things, actually. This week we start digging into an amazing example of comradery and the blessings that come from walking life's path with faithful friends.

Here's what to expect this week:

- **Day 1: Jesus Goes Viral**
  Four ordinary men give us an example of the power of faith and friendship.

- **Day 2: The Blessing of Saying "Yes"**
  Good things await those who follow Jesus.

- **Day 3: The Little Things**
  Small acts of obedience done in faith lead to big results.

To get us all on the same foot as we take off on our journey, please **READ** Mark 2:1-12.

This is one of those visual stories that almost demands a felt board! For those of you who grew up going to Sunday School way back in the day, don't you remember sitting on the rug, crisscross applesauce, in front of that green flannel? I have memories of hoping my teacher Mrs. Judy would call my name to put "felt Jesus" in the right spot on the board. I can still visualize the scowls of the religious men and the four men carrying the mat.

Let's set the stage for our story with a few things:

Based on Mark 2, describe the situation at the house where Jesus was teaching.

The house was crowded, to say the least. People squeezing around the door and peeking through windows. I wonder what it looked like or felt like or even smelled like inside the house. All those people! And no deodorant!

And think on this: houses in biblical times were typically built of stone and had flat roofs made of mud mixed with straw. There was usually an exterior staircase that led from the ground to the top of the roof.[1]

Take a minute to draw a house in the frame that looks like the description. Don't worry. You won't be graded on your artistic flair. Keep it simple.

Well done! Keep this visual in your mind as we discover what happened in the days leading up to this crowded scene. To do this, we are going to back up a chapter to Mark 1.

READ Mark 1:29-31. (Keep your Bible open. We will be reading further.)

What happened?

READ Mark 1:32-34.

Who was brought to Jesus for healing?

Look again at Mark1:33. The whole town gathered at the door to watch. The word was spreading. Jesus was developing a following.

But the miracles continue! **READ** Mark 1: 40-42.

What was the man healed from?

- ❑ Demon possession
- ❑ High fever
- ❑ Leprosy
- ❑ Blindness

Now we return to our original story. Mark 2:1 says, *"When Jesus returned to Capernaum several days later, the news spread quickly…"*

Can't you just feel the excitement? Jesus is back in town. He's been all over the region healing people of all kinds of illnesses and ailments…even demon possession. That type of news spreads faster than wildfire, especially when doctors and medicine were hard to come by and, even if you could afford them, they were limited by the knowledge of the day. Can you imagine the desperation of those in need of healing, both physically and spiritually?

This despair, in part, drove the crowds to gather at the stone house. People hung from the rafters just to hear one word from this carpenter turned healer, Jesus.

At this time, four men arrive at the house grasping tightly to four corners of a mat carrying their paralyzed friend and hoping to get him to this man of miracles. I can almost hear their excited conversation with each other…*Surely if he can heal leprosy, he can help our friend walk!*

Undeterred by the blocked doorways and windows, the friends devise a plan. Up the stairs! Through the roof! Lower him down!

READ Mark 2:5 and fill in the blank.

Seeing ___________ faith, Jesus said to the paralyzed man, "My child, your sins are forgiven."

"Their" faith. That one word forever changed the way I view friendship. Because of the faith of the friends, Jesus healed the paralyzed man, both spiritually and physically. It was **not** the faith of the healed one, but the faith of his friends. Let that sink in for a moment then answer these questions.

Do you have some faithful friends in your life who would stop at nothing to get you to the feet of Jesus? If so, let's name some names and give thanks.

If your answer is no, start praying for God to bless you with friends like these. Then keep praying.

For me, the answer to this question is a very thankful and humble, "Yes!" In my early thirties when I was living in Jacksonville, I had a medical emergency. After speaking with the nurse over the phone and asking a neighbor to watch my young boys, I drove myself to the hospital. My husband was out of the country and since I am independent to a fault, I thought an ambulance was completely unnecessary. Sigh.

Things progressed rapidly once I got to the emergency room. Paperwork, questions, and scans, followed by me fainting in a hallway. I had an ectopic pregnancy, and I needed surgery immediately. I vaguely remember my friends April, Maureen, and Cory being bedside as the doctor tried to explain what was about to happen. The next thing I knew; I was waking up from surgery with my sweet husband's face gazing down upon me.

What I would later find out is that these three friends dropped everything and were at the hospital during the entire ordeal praying for me nonstop. They prayed for my husband to get there safely, they prayed for the medical team, they prayed for my family, they prayed for my broken heart, and they prayed for Jesus to spare my very life.

That, my dear ones, is friendship! I give thanks all the time for these precious ladies and I pray for every last one of us to have friends like that.

And pray in the Spirit on all occasions with all kinds of prayers and requests. With this in mind, be alert and always keep on praying for all the Lord's people.

EPHESIANS 6:18

But here's the harder question. Are you this type of friend?

Are you willing to go above and beyond to deliver your friends to the feet of the only One who can truly heal and save and forgive? Would Jesus see **your** faith and be moved to act?

May it be said of me, Lord. May it be said of each one of us! In the mighty name of Jesus I pray.

Let's end today with a few verses on friendship.

> *Likewise, two people lying close together can keep each other warm. But how can one be warm alone? A person standing alone can be attacked and defeated, but two can stand back-to-back and conquer. Three are even better, for a triple-braided cord is not easily broken (Ecclesiastes 4:11-12, NLT).*
>
> *This is my command: Love one another the way I loved you. This is the very best way to love. Put your life on the line for your friends (John 15:12-13, MSG).*
>
> *Friends love through all kinds of weather (Proverbs 17:17a, MSG).*
>
> *The righteous choose their friends carefully, but the way of the wicked leads them astray (Proverbs 12:26, NIV).*

Circle one that speaks to you. Then pray about it and meditate on it this week.

Day 2

THE BLESSING OF "YES"

We are going to start today with a prayer.

Heavenly Father, be with us today as we study your Word. Send your Holy Spirit to teach us what you want us to know and put into practice. Our hearts and minds are yours. In the name of Jesus. Amen.

READ Mark 2:1-12 one more time. As you read, make a mental note of all the different people who were there that day.

Who was at the crowded house?

That's a lot of people. Today we are going to focus on a few different ones: the homeowner, the Pharisees, and the people in the crowd.

The homeowner. What do we know about him from reading the passage? Really give it some thought, then write down some of the possibilities.

You could have written down a few suppositions: the homeowner was hospitable, or he had an open heart and mind towards Jesus, or you could've written that we don't know much from the passage in Mark. But this miracle of Jesus is also written down in the book of

Luke 5:17-26. If we look at Luke's accounting of the story…nope. Nothing. No mention of him.

So why are we focusing on this invisible homeowner? Here's why: He said yes to Jesus. Well…we know he at least said yes to Jesus staying at his home. Mark 2:2 states, "Soon the house where he was staying was so packed with visitors…" Then later on in the story, if you remember, the man's roof ends up with a man-sized hole in it.

What do you imagine would be going through your mind if you were the homeowner in this situation?

I can only imagine what some of your answers are!

Because we are humans and come in all types of temperaments, we will never know this side of heaven what he thought or did during the commotion. But here's some food for thought…after he witnessed the day's events, after he saw the paralyzed man get up and walk out at the command of Jesus….do you think he was:

- Fretting over the crowd in his house?
- Worrying about the damage to his roof?
- Siding with the religious leaders?
- Standing in awe and wonder at what he had just witnessed?

I don't know about you, but I would like to think it was the last one. His house was the scene of a miracle of the Lord! Can you imagine how many times he told that story to his family and grandchildren? He probably told it to anyone who would listen!

Has there been a time when you witnessed something that only God could do and you just couldn't wait to tell someone?

If so, give a few details.

One thought that resonated with me was that serving God can be messy. The homeowner literally "opened up his home" to the neighborhood and ended up with all the broken furniture to show for it. But he also ended up with a story to tell.

I'm going to ask you a few yes or no questions. If you can answer yes to any of these, circle the question.

> Can you let go of expectations and do something God is asking of you even if you don't know the outcome?
>
> If things get messy in the middle of the "doing", will your obedience remain consistent?
>
> Are you willing, like the homeowner, to let go of control and let God do His thing…His way?

Ooooooh, sister. Those are some tough questions, but they are definitely worth spending some time in prayer.

Let's move on to the "teachers of religious law."

> *But some of the teachers of religious law who were sitting there thought to themselves, "What is he saying? This is blasphemy! Only God can forgive sins!" (Mark 2:6-7).*

These religious leaders were appalled. They could not believe that Jesus was asserting himself as the Son of God. They knew that anyone who claimed to have the power or right to forgive sins is making himself equal to God. They refused to see Jesus for who he was…the long-awaited Messiah.[2]

Jesus had plenty of experiences with religious authorities. Let's look up the following:

Luke 6:1-5

Why are the Pharisees upset with Jesus ?

Luke 6:6-11

What are they mad about this time ?

Take a minute to consider this: the naysayers in the latter example are literally watching a miracle take place in front of their very eyes, yet this act of Jesus fills them with rage (Luke 6:11).

Do you have naysayers in your life who put down your faith?

If so, let's name some names.

Now, let's pray for them by name. Pray for the Holy Spirit to soften their hearts towards God and give you favor with them. Go ahead. We'll wait for each other.

I love the final verse of our "Four Friends" story.

> *And the man jumped up, grabbed his mat, and walked out through the stunned onlookers. They were all amazed and praised God, exclaiming, "We've never seen anything like this before!" (Mark 2:12).*

Oh, to be a person in that crowded house! They witnessed at least two spectacular acts of God that day…they saw someone made whole spiritually and physically.

What does it take to be a witness?

The Merriam-Webster dictionary states that a witness is "one who has personal knowledge of something."[3]

Every person in that packed house had personal knowledge of Jesus from that day forward. Don't think for a minute those witnesses ever forgot what they saw!

And what did they do with what they saw? Mark 2:12 has your answer: They praised God.

Do you know someone who has witnessed a miracle?

If so, they must've told you about it. Did the hearing of the story bless you? Praising God for His faithfulness and goodness in our lives is so important!

Why is it important to tell others what God has done?

READ Psalm 40:1-3 in the margin for the answer.

I waited patiently for the Lord to help me, and he turned to me and heard my cry.

He lifted me out of the pit of despair, out of the mud and the mire. He set my feet on solid ground and steadied me as I walked along.

He has given me a new song to sing, a hymn of praise to our God. Many will see what he has done and be amazed. They will put their trust in the Lord.

PSALM 40:1-3

Think about the four friends, the homeowner, the Pharisees, and the people in the crowd…who do you want to be? Choose as many as you like.

- ❑ The faithful friends who stopped at nothing to get their loved one to Jesus.
- ❑ The homeowner who welcomed Jesus into his home no matter the consequences.
- ❑ The Pharisees who couldn't see the goodness and love of God when it was right in front of them.
- ❑ The witnesses who praised God exclaiming, "We've never seen anything like this before!"

Make no mistake. We have a choice in who we are going to be.

Make no mistake. We have a choice in who we are going to be.

The four men said yes to their faith and no to the obstacles. They were getting to Jesus. Period.

The homeowner said yes to Jesus, and he had a story to tell the rest of his life. His home was the scene of Jesus proving Himself as the Son of God and the Son of Man.

Every person in the crowd said yes to showing up that day. They went away praising God and opening up hearts with every retelling of the story.

Say yes to Jesus today. Say yes, and He will show you the miraculous.

If you're ready to take that step into following Jesus, say a prayer right now.

> *God, I am ready for you to take over my life. I accept your Son Jesus and believe that He died on the cross for my sins, He rose again, and He is now with you in heaven.*
>
> *Forgive me, Lord, for all my sins. Thank you that I now get to be with you forever. Please give me what I need to live for you.*

I am yours.

In the name of Jesus, Amen.

Congratulations! You are now in the family of God. If you just prayed this for the first time, let someone know. Reach out to a friend who knows and loves Jesus. You need someone to talk to, pray with, and answer questions. We are all in this together!

Day 3
THE LITTLE THINGS

Buckle up, sisters! The homework today is a call to action, but please don't let that scare you. This is something we can all do. And here's the good news: its world changing. Let's get going, shall we?

Today we are going to take a look at the four men and dial into their actions. Take a moment to imagine what the sequence of events might have been for those helpful friends that day.

I know you've read this passage several times, but for old times' sake, please go over Mark 2:1-12 one more time.

So, my dear brothers and sisters, be strong and immovable. Always work enthusiastically for the Lord, for you know that nothing you do for the Lord is ever useless.

1 CORINTHIANS 15:58

Make a list of action words the four men had to complete in order to get their friend to the feet of Jesus. (Example: hoisted)

Can you visualize all the steps they had to complete?

When the four friends started out carrying their paralyzed pal, they may not have foreseen all the difficulties that lay ahead. I don't know about you, but the crowd may have made me change my mind. I mean, I won't drive downtown for anything if there's a slight chance I'll get stuck in traffic. Anyone with me?

These men kept going. Nothing was going to get in their way…not even a roof! And think about this:

- Where did the rope come from?
- Did they have one with them or did someone have to go find one while the others waited in the hot sun?

- Did they consider the damage to the house or did they dive right in?
- Did they all agree that this was a good idea?

All of these questions have been on my mind for years. But here's the one I really want to ask:

- Did the friends consider their actions an amazing feat or would they simply say, "Awww…it wasn't much. We just wanted to help our friend."

Let's look at a few more biblical examples of people who did something for Jesus.

READ John 6:1-13.

What did the boy give to Jesus?

What did Jesus do with his offering?

Do you think the boy ever forgot what he witnessed? YES or NO

READ John 2:1-10.

Who did Jesus ask for help?

What did he ask of them?

Do you think the servants ever forgot what they saw? YES or NO

The little boy was asked to give what he had. The servants were asked for some water. The four men took their friend to Jesus.

In the hands of God, our small offerings are used for eternal significance.

Ordinary things, big miracles. In the hands of God, our small offerings are used for eternal significance.

Many years ago when I was living in Colorado, I was a part of the Women's Leadership Team at church. I was in charge of hospitality, which is a fancy way of saying I showed up early to events and made sure we had plenty of coffee. Caffeine is very important, especially for a morning study!

One of the women on the team, Brenda, was an amazing example of boldness and kindness. She mentioned at one of our planning meetings how she invites women to our upcoming studies. She drafts an email invitation and sends it out to her new neighbors or moms at her children's school.

Our people must learn to devote themselves to doing what is good, in order to provide for urgent needs and not live unproductive lives.

TITUS 3:14

"Well," I thought. "If Brenda can do it, I can do it." I thought of a dozen moms from my kids' elementary school I could invite. But here's the problem. I had never been that bold before. Send an email to women I don't know that well? What will they think? What if they say no? Is this weird?

I typed up the email and hovered over the send button for a minute or two. With fear and trepidation, I closed my eyes, said a prayer, and sent it. To my surprise, three women said yes and actually attended the Bible study. Two of them brought their moms! Years later, one of those women was baptized at the church and she named me by name in her testimony!

People…I sent an email. God took my fearful, full of doubt, tiny act of obedience and used it to get this amazing woman into eternal friendship with Him. Sometimes it's the little things.

Let's brainstorm. What are some "little things" you can do for God?

Today:

This week:

God can take the smallest gesture and turn it into a life changer! He takes the little that we give Him, and He multiplies it beyond our wildest dreams.

Pray for God to show you what He wants you to do. Pray for Him to give you everything you need to do it. Now do it!!! Take that step of faith and then watch as He multiplies your gift for His glory. You will never forget what you witness.

Friendship Lesson:

Bring your friends to the feet of Jesus.

Live It Out:

How are you going to apply what you've learned this week to your own life?

Prayer:

Heavenly Father, thank you for your Word. Place the lessons from this week firmly in my heart. Strengthen my faith so that you will be glorified and others will see you in me. Give me everything I need to be a faithful friend. In the Mighty Name of Jesus, Amen.

Session 1: "The Four Friends" Video Notes

Do NOT feel the need to go in order or fit all the questions into the time allotted. Each woman should choose at least one of the questions to ask in her small group. Then get to talking and sharing your hearts with each other!

1. What would you do if you had an hour of free time?
2. Describe an unconventional solution to a problem you've encountered.
3. Whom do you want to bring to the feet of Jesus right now?
4. What is your favorite miracle in the Bible?
5. What do you need in a friend during this season of life?
6. What is a dream you're hoping will come true?
7. Have you ever witnessed a miracle? Share it with the group.
8. What are you most grateful for in your life?
9. When have you felt the most challenged?
10. What's the most beautiful place you've ever been?

Prayer Requests:

Week Two

MARY & ELIZABETH

I recently took my teenage daughter to a large extended family event out of state. She was not familiar with this side of our family tree. Sure, they were related, but virtually strangers, at the same time. I reassured her that she would like them and that they already loved her. Skeptical one, that girl though. However, once we arrived, it didn't take long for her to feel like she belonged. They even threw her a surprise 16th birthday party. The thing about relatives is that it doesn't matter how many years you've spent apart, as soon as you are together again, the years fall away quickly. You feel "at home" sharing space with each other.

Luke tells the story of two other distant relatives, Elizabeth and Mary, which we will examine this week.

- **Day 1: Positive Pregnancy Tests**
  Angelic visitations rock Elizabeth and Mary's world.

- **Day 2: Undeniable Miracles**
  Faith precedes the miraculous.

- **Day 3: The Equipping**
  Find a mentor and be a mentor.

Day 1

POSITIVE PREGNANCY TESTS

We have some reading today. Stay with me.

READ Luke 1:5-25 and fill in the blanks for Luke 1:6-7.

"Zechariah and Elizabeth were ______________________________
in God's eyes, careful to _______ all of the Lord's ________________
and __________________."

Glance at verses 7 and 18. How did Luke describe Elizabeth's age?
____(ouch!)

Friend, although difficult to endure, suffering does have a way of bringing out the best in us IF we let it.

Elizabeth had been unable to conceive for a very long time. Infertility is an extremely painful experience for many women, but in this time and place, it was especially challenging. Imagine no doctors who could run tests and provide answers to your questions! No surrogacy options. No adoption agencies. And of course the stigma that went along with infertility at the time—as women cursed by God. My heart breaks for them!

All of this amounts to years of pain and suffering for Elizabeth. And yet…she was righteous in God's eyes.

Friend, although difficult to endure, suffering does have a way of bringing out the best in us IF we let it. There is a refining fire that burns away the parts of our heart that are far away from God, until all we have is Him to get us through. It is then that we learn He is enough. Always has been. Always will be. Elizabeth had let the Lord do a great work in her heart.

We get insight into Elizabeth's thoughts about her pregnancy in Luke 1:25.

> *"How kind the Lord is!" she exclaimed. "He has taken away my disgrace of having no children."*

Elizabeth had let the Lord do a great work in her heart.

She described the Lord as kind or favored, depending on your translation. I can think of some other thoughts that she, or should I say I, might have had...

It's about time! Where have you been God?

Why couldn't you do this 30 years ago?

But God knew Elizabeth's heart was full of faith.

Friend, we have all experienced disappointments in this life, but we can be like Elizabeth and continue to walk in faith. Is there an area of your life that you need to allow God to do a great work in your heart? Share it below.

Literally, stop right now, set a timer for 60 seconds and spend it in prayer asking God to bless that area of your heart and life.

Even though this exciting, unexpected, long-prayed-for baby was now on his way, Elizabeth spent the first five months in seclusion (Luke 1: 24). She obviously wasn't broadcasting it from the rooftops.

Don't you wonder why she stayed in seclusion? Maybe she was worried she would lose the child? After so many years of trying to conceive, it's hard to believe there wasn't some level of fear there. Or maybe she didn't want to give an opportunity to those who whispered about her infertility for all those years to steal her joy again. Or maybe she just wanted to enjoy this gift from the hand of her *kind* Father in secret.

Whatever her reason, this secret had an expiration date!

Elizabeth's much younger relative, Mary, was about to get a press release straight from Gabriel, who "stands in the very presence of God!" (Luke 1:19).

Let's read with fresh eyes Gabriel's message to Mary.

READ Luke 1:26-38.

Although we are not given an exact age, we can infer that Mary was young. She was betrothed to Joseph already, and in Jewish custom and culture, she would have been a teenager.[1]

"In Jewish culture then a man and woman were betrothed or pledged to each other for a period of time before the actual consummation of their marriage. This betrothal was much stronger than an engagement period today, for the two were considered husband and wife except that they did not live together till after the wedding."[2]

Mary and Joseph were in this betrothal stage, when Mary gets an angelic visitor who shares the amazing news that she has been chosen to bear the Son of God, even though she is a virgin. If you were Mary, which of these emotions do you think you would have felt?

- ❑ Excited
- ❑ Humbled
- ❑ Terrified
- ❑ Worried
- ❑ Uncertain

I think I would have felt all of them!

We don't know if Mary shared this amazing news with anyone right away. We do know she felt the need to see the one person Gabriel mentioned, Elizabeth. "A sign in the Old Testament was often associated with a confirming observable phenomenon which accompanied a word of prophecy."[3] Elizabeth's pregnancy would be her sign of confirmation!

It makes sense. If you received a prophetic message via angel, of something that had literally NEVER happened to anyone else, wouldn't you want some additional confirmation?

To me, it makes perfect sense to go to Elizabeth first and verify Gabriel's message.

How far into the pregnancy was Elizabeth when Gabriel appeared to Mary? (Luke 1:26, 36).

- ❑ 3 months
- ❑ 6 months
- ❑ 8 months

Mary would know at first sight if Elizabeth had a 6-month bun in the oven.

READ Luke 1:39. How long did Mary wait before she left to go visit Elizabeth?

- ❑ A few days
- ❑ A few weeks
- ❑ A few months

Have you ever felt like God has spoken something to your heart and then used someone else to confirm it for you? Describe it briefly in the margin.

Although we can't demand God confirm things for us all the time, there are times, in His grace, when He does.

I had a long-term boyfriend through high school and into college. He was truly a great guy. I clearly remember making the decision one weekend in the quiet recesses of my heart that he was "it" for me…the man I wanted to marry and spend my life with. Then within days, I felt the Holy Spirit impress upon me that I was to break up with him. I didn't understand. Why? He was a strong Christian who loved me and I loved him. Why would God ask this of me? I couldn't make sense of it, so I prayed, "God, if this is something you really want me to do, then I will need you to confirm it for me. I will ask the two people I trust the most in the world, my mom and my best friend, and I need you to confirm this break-up through them."

Well, long story short…they both did. Even using the exact same words and phrases as each other. I was heart-broken. I didn't want to hurt him and I didn't want to end it. But God had kept up His part of the bargain, so I had to keep up mine. Looking back, I can see why God put my feet on a different path, but hindsight is always 20/20. Although we can't demand God confirm things for us all the time, there are times, in His grace, when He does.

Mary is about to experience one of those times herself. We will pick up with her and Elizabeth's remarkable reunion in our next lesson. Until then, take some time to contemplate the unexpected turns in your life, and how God has used them for your good.

WRITE a quick thank you note to the Lord for guiding your steps.

Day 2

UNDENIABLE MIRACLES

Two distant relatives, brought together by some amazing similarities. Both Elizabeth and Mary had:

- Found favor with God
- Miraculous pregnancies
- Pregnancies foretold by the angel Gabriel
- The names of their sons given to them by God
- Prophetic words spoken over their children

Even though they were related, these two women were decades and miles apart. Nazareth and the hill country of Judea were over 80 miles away from each other…back before planes, trains, and automobiles (see fig. 1). That's a hike. Literally. One I'm sure they didn't make frequently. However, their lives were about to seriously intersect.

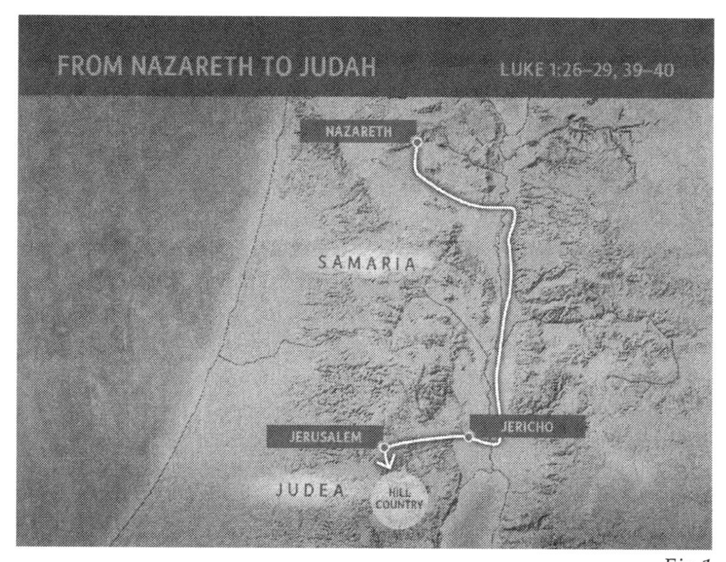

Fig.1

When Mary finally arrived, she must have been both physically and mentally exhausted from her nearly weeklong journey. I imagine she spent the trip contemplating all the areas of her life that were going to change. What would Joseph do? Would he leave her? What would her friends and family think? Surely, anxiety was an unwelcome companion. Yet, even considering all the challenges ahead, she must have also been ready to burst from holding in a secret destined to change the world forever.

Let's break out our Bibles again.

READ Luke 1:39-45.

When Mary walks into the house, baby John leapt in Elizabeth's womb, and Elizabeth was filled with the Holy Spirit. Can you imagine Mary's thoughts and feelings at hearing the following words from Elizabeth as a greeting?

> *"God has blessed you above all women, and your child is blessed. Why am I so honored, that the mother of my Lord should visit me? When I heard your greeting, the baby in my womb jumped for joy. You are blessed because you believed that the Lord would do what he said" (Luke 1:42-43).*

How do you think hearing these words made Mary feel?

The prophecy from Gabriel was confirmed the **moment** she walked in the door; by Elizabeth's pregnancy bump and by her prophetic words to Mary.

Mary then burst into a song of praise. I encourage you to say or sing her words aloud the way you think Mary might have!

READ Luke 1:46-55.

"The purely personal expression of the glad emotions awakened by Elisabeth's [sic] presence and salutation, which came to Mary as confirmation of the angel's annunciation. Not when Gabriel spoke, but when a woman like herself called her 'mother of my Lord,' did she break into praise. There is a deep truth there. God's voice is made more sure to our weakness when it is echoed by human lips, and our inmost hopes attain substance when they are shared and spoken by another…Her first words are a burst of rapturous and wondering praise, in which the full heart runs over. Silence is impossible, and speech a relief."[4]

I can only imagine the joy they both felt. It truly flowed out of them. If human beings were bursting with excitement about this news, can you imagine the scene in the spiritual realm? God, Jesus and The Holy Spirit all knew the significance of this moment. Before Eve's first bite of the apple, the plan was in place, and now the beginning credits start to roll. Jesus, one of the Triune Godhead was taking his place, in the womb of a teenager. He was giving up his divine privileges and humbling himself in obedience to God, His father.[5] Salvation and restoration for God's children were within reach. No, this excitement was not limited to mortals; the Holy Spirit left His imprint of joy all over this story.

How did the Holy Spirit show up in the following verses?

Luke 1:13-15

Luke 1:35

Luke 1:41

As modern day Christians, we experience the permanent indwelling of the Holy Spirit as soon as we accept Jesus as Lord. However, in the Old Testament, many scholars believe the Holy Spirit within a believer was "selective and temporary," not a guarantee.[6] So much about this whole story is extraordinary and rare, but this part…this overflowing of the Holy Spirit, is something WE can experience!

As modern day Christians, we experience the permanent indwelling of the Holy Spirit as soon as we accept Jesus as Lord.

There are times when the Holy Spirit's presence is undeniable. If you've had an experience like that, what was your reaction? Share it below.

As a single mom, there have been many times when finances were tight, so saving for my children's college seemed out of reach. Whenever the topic would come up, my consistent response was that God would provide…as He had so many times before. I never anticipated how He would do it; I just believed He would. Then, when my daughter was a senior in high school, it happened. The Holy Spirit started moving mightily! A relationship was restored, which led to a conversation revealing an unknown option to us. I felt like we were on the cusp of a miracle! We pursued it and ended up getting 100% of her tuition, housing, food, and books covered, in a way we never would have expected! I could just feel the Holy Spirt's presence when the news came in…and you had better believe I shouted for joy! My prayer is that we all have those experiences where it could be "only God!"

However, my friends, there is usually something that precedes those miracles…faith. It's true for my story, but it also is found in both Mary and Elizabeth's examples.

I want to challenge you to answer this question. Do I have the kind of faith that precedes the miraculous?

Please understand I am not saying you aren't receiving a much-prayed-for miracle because of a lack of faith. I don't believe God is a slot machine, where we put in faith and hit the jackpot every time. I am saying there is something to us trusting God and believing He doesn't withhold good from His children. His plan for you is the best plan, whatever it is.

Ask God for a fresh anointing of faith in your life. Here are a few suggestions as to how:

- Make a list of all the ways God has been faithful to you. Once we see in black and white how trustworthy He has been in our past, it becomes easier to believe He will be faithful in the future.

- Get on your knees (literally, if you are able) and ask God for a renewed faith and trust in **His** plan for your life.

- Memorize Hebrews 11:6: "And it is impossible to please God without faith. Anyone who wants to come to him must believe that God exists and that he rewards those who sincerely seek him." God rewards those who come to Him with believing hearts. Keep sincerely seeking Him.

God rewards those who come to Him with believing hearts.

Day 3
THE EQUIPPING

Let's begin today with the last mention of Mary and Elizabeth's time together.

> *Mary stayed with Elizabeth for three months and then returned home (Luke 1:56).*

Three months. That's enough time for the shock to wear off, but for the morning sickness to set in! God knew Mary needed to be in a safe place, loved and encouraged, during this important stage of her pregnancy. And I'm sure Elizabeth appreciated the help with daily tasks as her womb (and joints) swelled.

What kind of conversations do you think they had? They were both first time moms. Did they share pregnancy woes? Morning sickness remedies? Did they tell the stories over and over to each other about Gabriel's messages? Assuming Zecharias wrote it out for Elizabeth…since according to Luke, the man wouldn't speak a word until John's birth. Yet another grace of God bringing these two women together…they had a lot to say…and no one else who could relate!

It's not a giant leap to guess that Mary considered Elizabeth a spiritual mentor. God doesn't waste anything. All those years in the desert, literally and figuratively, gave Elizabeth a well of wisdom to draw from, which was just what Mary needed at that time.

A mentor is defined as "an experienced and trusted advisor."[7] I'm sure Elizabeth fit the bill in this area. Unfortunately, she had experienced enough heartache and the whispers of others for a lifetime…and Mary would be heading into a similar storm. A young girl, not officially married, but pregnant. Rumors would be fierce! I believe her time with Elizabeth helped equip her for what was coming.

Although many mentors may be older than you, age is not as important as experience and wisdom. If you've been through something, and I don't know anyone who makes it through this life without challenges, you are capable of helping or mentoring someone else. Friend…someone needs you!

READ 2 Corinthians 1:4 in the margin.

He comforts us in all our troubles so that we can comfort others. When they are troubled, we will be able to give them the same comfort God has given us.

2 CORINTHIANS 1:4

This life isn't easy. It wasn't for Elizabeth. It wasn't for Mary. And it isn't for us. However, we can help each other by sharing our hearts and lives authentically with others.

God calls us and then He equips us. Many times, He uses other people in our lives to help us get through hardships. When my daughter was first diagnosed with autism, I joined a local gathering of parents with children on the spectrum. The leaders of the group were ahead of me in the journey and had wisdom to impart. We would meet monthly and learn about new therapies, how to get resources, and share our experiences. I learned so much through those meetings. They helped prepare me to advocate for my daughter in better ways than I would have been able to do on my own.

Is there an area in your life where you feel ill equipped and could use some good counsel? List it below.

Take a moment and brainstorm. Do you know someone who has already been through something similar? Could you research and see if there are any local or church connection groups, which would address this topic? List any ideas you have. Go ahead and Google it if you need to. We'll wait.

After Gabriel told Mary about Elizabeth's surprise pregnancy, Mary could have had the *idea* to go see Elizabeth, but then not followed through on it. However, if she had stayed home, she would have missed all the blessings and the preparation God had planned for her.

Sometimes we get an idea from the Lord and have to make a choice. Are we going to go through with it, even if it pushes us out of our comfort zone? Make a promise to yourself (and God) to pursue wisdom and take the next steps of obedience.

What next step is He asking you to take?

Ask God for faithful friends and mentors in your life...but the best way to find them is to become one yourself.

When Mary went home, she knew Elizabeth was in her corner, supporting and praying for her.

Do you have anyone like that in your corner? Identify the "Elizabeths" in your life?

Identify who your "Marys" are?

Ask God for faithful friends and mentors in your life...but the best way to find them is to become one yourself. Seek to serve others and believe God will bless you with authentic and real relationships!

Friendship Lesson:

Have a mentor and be a mentor.

Live It Out:

How are you going to apply what you've learned this week to your own life?

Prayer:

Dear Heavenly Father, thank you for the women you have placed in my life who have encouraged and mentored me. Help me to pass that gift along. Give me eyes to see the women you have placed in my life and how I might be an encourager to them. Amen.

Session 2: "Mary & Elizabeth" Video Notes

Friendship Builder Questions

Do NOT feel the need to go in order or fit all the questions into the time allotted. Each woman should choose at least one of the questions to ask in her small group. Then get to talking and sharing your hearts with each other!

1. Out of all your family members, who are you closest to and why?
2. Have you experienced an angel encounter?
3. How do you cope with stress?
4. Would you rather have a mentor or be a mentor? Why?
5. What would your dream vacation consist of?
6. In what area do you feel like you have experience that could help someone else?
7. What is your favorite way to spend a Saturday?
8. Who do you look up to the most, and what qualities do you love about that person?
9. When you have a problem, do you fix it yourself or ask for help?
10. Have you ever been the victim of rumors? How did you handle it?

Prayer Requests:

Week Three

JONATHAN & DAVID

A king's throne, murderous plots, deception, family drama, and running from authorities. This may sound like a reality show, when in fact, these are glimpses into Jonathan and David's story! Unfortunately, we cannot tackle this entire dramatic saga in one week, but I encourage you to dig deeper and spend some time reading about the rise and fall of Jonathan's father, King Saul, and the unlikely shepherd boy chosen as a king. What we will dig into this week is the surprising friendship that develops between Jonathan and David.

God uses friendships as a way to bless us and to accomplish His purposes. Jonathan and David had a fiercely loyal, selfless, faithful, and inspiring friendship that stood the test of time. Let's get to know them a bit this week and see how we might build a friendship like theirs.

- **Day 1: Covenant Friendship**
  Taking your friendships to a deeper level.

- **Day 2: Jealousy**
  Insecurity is the breeding ground for jealousy.

- **Day 3: Legacy**
  Leave a legacy of love and acts of kindness.

Day 1

COVENANT FRIENDSHIP

Isn't it true that few things in life are more important than having really good friends?

Our lesson this week focuses on one friendship in particular…that of Jonathan and David. Two men from different backgrounds but they had something meaningful in common. Today we will discover what that was.

Let's take a look at the very different lives of these unlikely friends.

Jonathan	David
A prince	A shepherd
Oldest son, in line to inherit the throne	Youngest of 8 sons
Tribe of Benjamin	Tribe of Judah
Grew up in a palace	Born in the little town of Bethlehem
Had his own armor	Had a harp and a slingshot

From a human perspective, it seems improbable that these two men would ever meet, much less become the best of friends. But God has a way of putting people together, doesn't He?

Let's look at how they met. **READ** 1 Samuel 17:45 – 18:4.

What famous encounter had just occurred?

David was receiving a hero's welcome after having just killed Goliath and helping win a great victory over the Philistines for Israel. Jonathan must have been impressed when he realized David was only a teenager! (1 Samuel 17:33). It was obvious David had not won by brute strength, but by faith in a God much greater than any giant.

Jonathan could relate. He had already proven he trusted God in battle when the odds were stacked against him. A few chapters before the story of David verses Goliath, we see Jonathan and his armor bearer go up against 20 Philistines. Final score Jonathan 20, Philistines 0.

READ the story in 1 Samuel 14:1-15.

Write, in your own words, what Jonathan says in 1 Samuel 14:6.

Jonathan stepped out in faith and proved he believed God for victory. Jonathan knew what trust in God was when he saw it, and David had it written all over him!

For all the differences these two men had, they shared a common bond of faith. Their friendship begins quickly and we are told that Jonathan makes a covenant with David.[1] So what does that mean?

In biblical times, when two people made a covenant, they swore an oath to fulfill certain obligations and at the same time, they received certain advantages from the relationship. When making this oath, God was invoked as a witness.[2]

God as a witness. That's serious and nothing to be taken lightly. Jonathan then proved his loyalty by giving David some very valuable items.

In 1 Samuel 18:4 what does Jonathan give David?

By giving David his royal garb, Jonathan was symbolically transferring his right to the throne to David.[3] What a confirmation for David that must have been. You see, Samuel had already quietly anointed David as the future king. God just keeps lining things up for His plan! Look at the timeline of events.

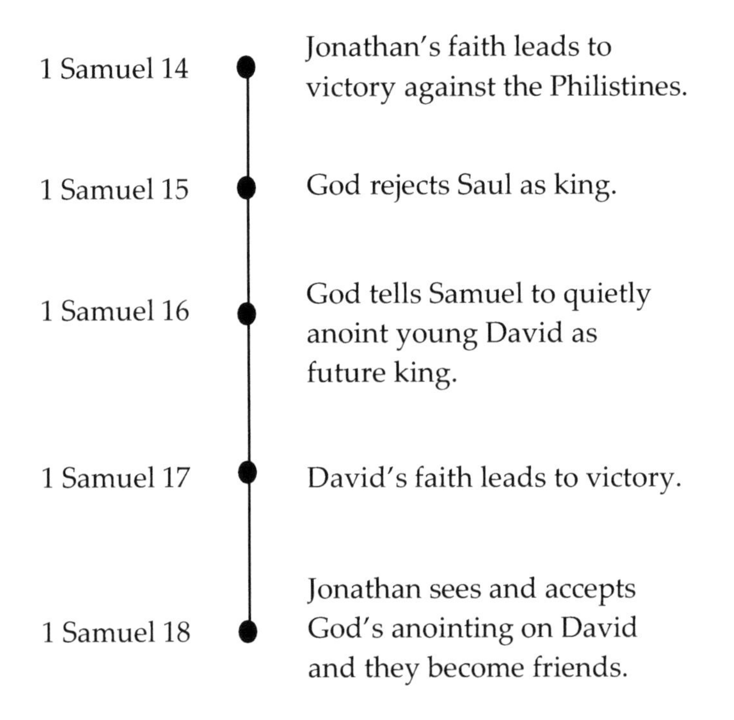

I have to say…Jonathan impresses me. His faith in God allows him to see David, not as a rival, but as a friend right from the start!

Think of your friendships. Have any of them started with an instant bond? If so, jot down a few memories.

I had this experience the first time I met April and Julie. We hit it off immediately and quickly discovered our shared faith. The Holy Spirit knit our hearts together from the very beginning. This friendship has stood the test of time and several cross-country moves. We love God before anyone or anything, and this keeps us lifting each other up and bringing each other back to God's Word when life creeps in and jades our thinking.

Over the years, God has taught us to do one other thing…pray for each other. Regularly. Out loud. For each other and with each other.

Look up James 5:16 and write it in the space provided.

There is something sacred about humbling ourselves, together, in front of God.

I love the NIRV version. *So confess your sins to one another. Pray for one another so that you might be healed. The prayer of a godly person is powerful. Things happen because of it.*

Underline the last two sentences.

Does that just make your heart race, or what? Things happen when godly people pray…when we share our weaknesses and pray for one another. There is something sacred about humbling ourselves, together, in front of God.

Have you ever prayed aloud with a friend? YES or NO

When you think about praying aloud with a friend, how does it make you feel?

- ❑ Unprepared
- ❑ Vulnerable
- ❑ Confident
- ❑ Scared
- ❑ Excited
- ❑ Anxious

Prayer Exercise: The next time you feel inclined to tell someone, "I'll pray for you"...instead ask them if it would be okay to pray for them right then. And then do it! They will walk away blessed...and so will you!

If you've never prayed together before, it might feel awkward at first. But if you're looking for a Jesus-centered, genuine friendship, it's worth the awkward. It's worth the step in faith to pray for each other. Remember...*the prayer of a godly person is powerful. Things happen because of i*t. I encourage you to challenge yourself to complete the Prayer Exercise listed in the margin and see how God moves!

What else does the Bible say about the qualities of a good friend? Look up the following verses and match them with the appropriate answer.

Proverbs 17:17	should love one another
Proverbs 12:26	a friend is always loyal
2 John 1:5	build each other up in faith
Jude 1:20	gives good advice

Loyalty, love, encouragement, wise counsel...great friends have godly traits.

Don't feel like you have to have it all together before starting the work of building a deep friendship!

A true friend is one that goes "in the trenches" with you. A person who is willing to get into the messy with you is one worth investing in. When I first met April, her life was messy. She was starting one of the darkest seasons of her life. Sharing, talking, and praying through the mess cemented our friendship. Don't feel like you have to have it all together before starting the work of building a deep friendship! True bonds of friendship are often formed or tested through some fiery trials.

Jonathan and David's friendship is about to face some of those, but we'll talk about that in our next day of homework. Until then, pray and meditate on the godly qualities of a good friend. Would these attributes describe you?

Day 2

OVERCOMING JEALOUSY

Although Jonathan and David start by becoming fast friends, their friendship is quickly tested when Jonathan's dad, King Saul, turns on David. We have a chunk of reading in today's homework, but stay with me. This story is too good to cut any of it out.

READ 1 Samuel 18:5-15.

Fill in the blank from verse 9.
"So from that time on Saul kept a ____________ eye on David."

It sure didn't take long from David's first introduction to the royal family before jealousy took hold. I can imagine Saul's blood starting to boil when he heard all the women of Israel singing:

"Saul has killed his thousands,
and David his ten thousands!"

Can you think of a time someone else got the accolades you thought you deserved? How did it make you feel?

What did Saul's jealousy lead him to do? (1 Samuel 18:10-11).

What did David do in response to Saul's attack?

- ❑ Hurl the spear back
- ❑ Escape…twice

I don't know about you, but one thing I'm looking forward to in heaven is not having any more insecurities!

This pattern of attempted murder and escape continues over and over again. Saul's desire to kill David became an obsession. Jealousy is born from insecurities, and Saul was worried he would lose his throne to this young, and already beloved, national hero.

In what areas of your life do you struggle with feeling insecure? Is it as a wife, mom, friend, in your appearance, or anything else?

Can you think of a time when your insecurities have held you back from something or caused you to do something you regret? List your example.

I don't know about you, but one thing I'm looking forward to in heaven is not having any more insecurities!

Let's look at how Jonathan and David's covenant friendship held up under the strain of these intense circumstances.

READ 1 Samuel 19:1-10.

What did Jonathan do in this passage? (Choose any that apply.)

- ❑ Agreed to assassinate David
- ❑ Told David what Saul was planning
- ❑ Influenced Saul to make peace with David
- ❑ Brought David back to serve in the king's court

Unfortunately, Jonathan's ability to negotiate peace for David with Saul was short-lived. I feel for Jonathan as he really was stuck in the middle of two important relationships in his life.

Have you ever been stuck in the middle, trying to navigate relationships? If so, between whom?

It would make sense if Jonathan had wanted David gone. With him out of the picture, Jonathan would have a clear line to the throne. While most men in Jonathan's situation may have felt jealous and threatened, Jonathan saw what God saw in David…Israel's next king!

Stay with me here. It's long, but reads like a series finale, with family drama and secret messages.

READ 1 Samuel 20 and then number these in the correct order of events.

______ David bows three times in front of Jonathan

______ Saul boils over in rage

______ Jonathan devises how to send a secret message to David

___1___ David proposes a plan to validate Saul's intent to kill him

______ Jonathan promises to talk to his father about David

______ The friends swear their loyalty and part ways

Jonathan proves his loyalty to David repeatedly, even when it cost him. "His [Jonathan] disinterestedness and willingness to surrender all claims to the throne for the sake of his friend gives evidence of a character that is unsurpassed."[4]

Proverbs 17:17 tells us "A friend loves at all times."

How should we feel about the calling God places on our friends' lives?

Let's be the kind of women who support each other's callings and celebrate successes together!

Let's be the kind of women who support each other's callings and celebrate successes together! Spend some time today thanking God for your friends and their accomplishments. If you find jealousy creeping in, ask God to take it from you and replace it with His love and joy.

Day 3

ACTS OF KINDNESS

Let's remind ourselves where we left Jonathan and David in our last day of homework.

READ 1 Samuel 20:42 below.

> *At last Jonathan said to David, "Go in peace, for we have sworn loyalty to each other in the Lord's name. The Lord is the witness of a bond between us and our children forever." Then David left, and Jonathan returned to the town.*

When they parted, they had no idea what the future held or whether they would ever see each other again.

When my family moved from Maryland to Florida, I was heartbroken over the friends I was leaving. I wondered if we would stay close with all the miles between us. I've been blessed to still see a few of these treasured friends regularly. We pick up right where we left off from the last time we were together! The time with them is even sweeter because I have such a deep appreciation for it and cherish every second that I get to spend with them now.

Do you have any friends that you don't get to see often but when you do, it's as if nothing has changed? If so, list their names.

Earlier this week we talked about praying with a friend. One of these friends might be a good place to start! These are precious relationships; hold tight to them! Treasure them because we don't know how long we will have them with us here on earth.

Let's look at Jonathan and David's last time together as recorded in Scriptures.

> *One day near Horesh, David received the news that Saul was on the way to Ziph to search for him and kill him. Jonathan went to find David and encouraged him to stay strong in his faith in God. "Don't be afraid," Jonathan reassured him. "My father will never find you! You are going to be the king of Israel, and I will be next to you, as my father, Saul, is well aware." So the two of them renewed their solemn pact before the LORD. Then Jonathan returned home, while David stayed at Horesh (1 Samuel 23:15-18).*

They were making plans for a future filled with possibilities, but it seems this was the last time they ever saw each other.

READ 2 Samuel 1:1-12.

How did Jonathan die?

How did David respond to the news of Jonathan's death?

A person's days are determined; you have decreed the number of his months and have set limits he cannot exceed.

JOB 14:5 (NIV)

In 2 Samuel 1:17-27, David, a musician, poured out his grief in a funeral song.

My husband and I struggled with infertility issues. When we had our second miscarriage, my heart was heavy with grief. On the same day, we were also scheduled to move to a new home. While I mourned in the hospital, my friends went to my house and started packing. This act of love left me forever changed. My friends gave me a legacy of love in action.

Although life went on without Jonathan, David made good on his solemn oath to his close friend.

READ 2 Samuel 9:1-13.

Draw lines to match the different characters with who they were.

Ziba	Son of Ammiel
Makir	Jonathan's son
Mephibosheth	Servant of Saul

In honor of Jonathan, David cared for his son, Mephibosheth (who was lame in both feet) like one of his own sons.

Have you ever been treated like family by someone not related to you? YES or NO

How did that make you feel?

Mephibosheth must have felt incredibly honored. Rather than dismissing someone with disabilities, David swoops in and shows kindness because of a promise he had made to his father. David even extends his kindness so far as to provide for Mephibosheth's future!

What did David invite Mephibosheth to do in 2 Samuel 9:13?

Remember during your school days when someone saved a seat just for you, maybe in the cafeteria or in the classroom. How did that make you feel?

My husband and I were called to fostering for four years with seven different children. We opened up a seat at our table and God allowed us to lavish love and kindness on those precious souls who needed

somewhere to belong. Those days were hard, but the rewards were oh so sweet!

This was David's heart for his friend's son. He wanted to protect him and do all he could to lavish kindness on him and give him hope. Jonathan's legacy of love and loyalty to David blessed his child, far into the future.

Friend, you have kindness to give! How can you express kindness and "save a seat" for someone today?

Daily actions add up to your life. Acts of kindness lead to a legacy of love. What kind of legacy do you want to leave?

Friendship Lesson:

Moving to deeper levels of friendship requires vulnerability.

Live it Out:

How are you going to apply what you've learned this week to your life?

Prayer:

Lord, thank you for this beautiful example of friendship, but most importantly, thank you for my friendship with you. Help me to understand my self-worth comes from knowing how deep your love is for me. Help me to be vulnerable and have deeper relationships so that I can receive all the blessings you have for me. In Jesus' Name, Amen.

Session 3: "Jonathan & David" Video Notes

Friendship Builder Questions

Do NOT feel the need to go in order or fit all the questions into the time allotted. Each woman should choose at least one of the questions to ask in her small group. Then get to talking and sharing your hearts with each other!

1. When was the last time you cried?
2. Share an act of kindness that impacted your life.
3. How do you like to celebrate your successes?
4. Have you overcome jealousy in any areas of your life?
5. What has been your hardest goodbye in life so far?
6. What's the bravest thing you can imagine doing?
7. How long is your oldest friendship?
8. Would you rather be a royal or have a royal as a best friend? (Put on your British caps!)
9. Where did you grow up?
10. What is a dream you've never said aloud?

Prayer Requests:

Julie Davis

Week Four

SARAI AND HAGAR

Get ready ladies. This week we are going to be learning lessons the hard way. One of the many things I love about the Bible is that the authors, inspired by God, held nothing back. They wrote about the good, the bad, and the excruciatingly ugly. No filters here.

Like everyone else, I love to learn lessons walking down easy street, but here's the hard truth: the most meaningful experiences of my walk with the Lord have happened in the middle of some really dark times. The difficult relationship we are studying this week could be combed over for months and we still wouldn't be finished learning the lessons. I chose this family because God taught me some significant lessons from them. Even when relationships are hard and don't work out, God is still working and moving for His glory and the good of His people. Are you ready? Good. Let's get going.

- **Day 1: Sarai**
  Waiting on God and His timing is always the best way forward.

- **Day 2: Hagar**
  Even in the midst of despair, God is with us and remains faithful.

- **Day 3: Promises Made, Promises Kept**
  God is faithful to keep His Word, even when relationships don't turn out the way we want.

Day 1
SARAI

It's complicated. That's how Sarai and Hagar would describe their relationship with Abram on all of their social media accounts. Sarai is the wife, while Hagar is the slave girl pregnant with Abram's son. Yikes. That's complicated, all right.

The people we are studying this week do not fit into the category of "friends," but looking at families found in the Bible provides valuable insight into relationships of all types.

All Scripture is inspired by God and is useful to teach us what is true and to make us realize what is wrong in our lives. It corrects us when we are wrong and teaches us to do what is right. God uses it to prepare and equip his people to do every good work.

2 TIMOTHY 3:16-17

READ Genesis 16 to get a grasp on the drama.

Whoo-eee! There is a lot going on in this family. God gives us a glimpse into these relationships, so we can learn from their triumphs and their failures, their faithfulness and their rebellion.

Let's remember that God uses everything in Scripture, and I mean everything, to teach us truth. This family's story is no different. Just to get our heads in the right place, read 2 Timothy 3:16-17 in the margin. With this in mind, we will continue with Genesis 16…Sarai, Abram, and Hagar.

First, let's look at the most appalling part of this passage. It seems absolutely beyond the realm of reason that Sarai would "give" her servant Hagar to her husband in an effort to have a son. However, this was a common practice of the day.

The NIV Cultural Backgrounds Study Bible explains it this way: "The solution proposed by Sarai is not as shocking or outlandish as it would seem to us today. In the ancient world, barrenness was a catastrophe because one of the primary roles of the family was to produce the next generation. The survival of the family line was of the highest value, and it depended on producing progeny. Whatever threat a second wife might pose to harmony in the family paled in comparison to the necessity of an heir being produced."[1]

So how did Abram, Sarai, and Hagar get to this point? To help us, let's look at Scripture to learn a few things about Abram:

- Genesis 12:1-3: God chose Abram to be the founding father of His people…the nation of Israel.
- Genesis 15:4-6: God promises Abram a son and that his descendants will be as numerous as the stars in the sky.

READ Genesis 13:2.

What else does this verse tell us about Abram?

With this little bit of background, we know that Abram is an extremely important part of God's plan.

But let's keep moving. What do we learn about Hagar? Place a check next to what we know to be true from Genesis 16.

- ❑ She is an Egyptian.
- ❑ She is a servant with little say in what happens to her.
- ❑ When she has the upper hand, she uses it.
- ❑ She runs away from her problems.
- ❑ She is obedient to what God tells her to do.

If you placed a check next to every one of these descriptions, well done! Hagar is all of these. When I linger on this list, I see myself too. I have boasted even though I know God loves humility. I have run away from problems only to have them come back with a vengeance. But I have also, at times, been obedient to what God has asked of me. Humans are soooo very complicated!

READ these verses written by the Apostle Paul in Romans 7:18-19:

> *And I know that nothing good lives in me, that is, in my sinful nature. I want to do what is right, but I can't. I want to do what is good, but I don't. I don't want to do what is wrong, but I do it anyway.*

Those verses hit me hard every time I read them. Someone as God-fearing and God-following as the Apostle Paul struggled with sin just like me! I don't know why that gives me comfort, but it does. Take a minute to rewrite Paul's thoughts in your own words.

Now let's put a spotlight on Sarai, Abram's wife. This is where we will spend the majority of our time today.

READ Genesis 12:14.

How is Sarai described in this verse? Choose the correct answer:

- ❑ She is trustworthy.
- ❑ She is young.
- ❑ She is beautiful.

Lots of people found Sarai attractive. We also know from reading Genesis 16 that Sarai is barren. What else can we glean about Sarai from this chapter?

Sarai blames others instead of taking responsibility, she doesn't treat others well (to say the least), and if you wrote down that Sarai was impatient…bingo.

Sarai knew that God had promised Abram a son. She believed the promise, but she got tired of waiting for God to make good on His Word.

Can you relate? Has there been a time in your life when "waiting on the Lord" got the better of you? Write down a few details.

I would love to say that patience is one of my virtues, but it's not. I actually had a trusted friend tell me one time that I was "getting ahead of the Holy Spirit." Did I listen to this wise counsel? No. I plowed ahead in my bullheadedness and reaped the consequences.

And so did Sarai.

What could Sarai have done differently?

- ❑ Prayed to God and asked for guidance.
- ❑ Had a good conversation with her husband about it.
- ❑ Recalled all the times God had been good to them.
- ❑ All of the above.

Instead of praying to God and waiting on a response, she took matters into her own hands. Instead of confiding in her husband, she trusted in her own emotions. Instead of reminding herself of all the times God was faithful, she devised a plan.

Sadly, Sarai's impatience didn't only affect her. Her decision and Abram's compliance had implications for many other people. No one sins in a bubble. The ramifications of what we do, for good or bad, often ripple through generations.

At the right time, I, the Lord, will make it happen.
ISAIAH 60:22

Before we close today's homework, read the verses in the margin. Then circle the one that speaks to you the most. Make an effort to memorize it this week. You will be surprised how often these words come back to you.

Be still in the presence of the Lord, and wait patiently for him to act.
PSALM 37:7

List below something you've been praying about but haven't received an answer from God yet.

In the morning, Lord, you hear my voice; in the morning I lay my requests before you and wait expectantly.
PSALM 5:3

Now ask God to help you learn to wait on Him and His timing.

I'm so proud of you for finishing this day of homework. It's been a tough one! But hang in there, sister. Learning more about God through His Word is always worth the effort. It's heart-mending, life-giving, and generation-changing.

Don't worry about anything; instead, pray about everything. Tell God what you need, and thank him for all he has done.
PHILIPPIANS 4:6

Day 2

HAGAR

Poor Hagar. The more I get to know her, the more compassion I have for this woman. I'm sure you felt it, too, during our first day of homework. Today we are going to take a closer look at this mistreated servant and learn some incredible lessons from an unlikely source.

READ Genesis 16 again and pay close attention to Hagar.

Use the following timeline to label the course of events:
(I've done the first one for you.)

Sarai is barren.
Hagar is given
to Abram.

In our work from Day 1, you will remember that the practice of a barren woman "giving" her servant as a wife to produce an heir was common. It seems strange and barbaric to us in the modern world. But here's another piece of information that will make you catch your breath:

The children born to Hagar would have been considered the children of Sarai.[2]

Hagar would have known this. Breaks your heart, doesn't it?

It's no wonder Hagar had contempt for her mistress once she discovered her pregnancy! I'm not condoning Hagar's attitude, but this does help explain it.

Let's look at someone else who acted out of emotion.

Peter, James, and John are with Jesus the night he is arrested. Judas betrays Jesus with a kiss, and a contingent of Roman soldiers and Temple guards are there to arrest Jesus.

READ John 18:10-11.

What did Peter do and how did Jesus respond to him? Choose the answer:

- ❑ Peter was asleep and Jesus had to wake him up.
- ❑ Peter denied Jesus and Jesus forgave him.
- ❑ Peter cut off the right ear of the high priest's slave and Jesus rebuked him.

At one point in Peter's life, he in fact did all of these things. In this passage though, he actually resorted to violence to protect Jesus. He grabbed a sword and cut off someone's ear! In my flawed reasoning, it's understandable under the circumstances. He was reacting in the moment to protect Jesus. But here's what we have to remember…we can't always trust our hearts to lead us to do the right thing.

Look up Jeremiah 17:9 and write it in the margin.

Yikes! *Lord, give me strength and wisdom to pause and pray before acting.*

In the case of Hagar and her attitude toward Sarai, it was the wrong action with an understandable motive. With Peter and his strong defense of Jesus, it was an understandable action but the wrong motive. Regardless, they were following their hearts rather than trusting God.

Think back to a time when you reacted to a person or situation in a way that may have been justifiable, but wasn't godly. Write down a few of the details.

Looking back, how would God have wanted you to react to the person or handle the situation? Look up the following verses and summarize them in the space provided.

Verse	Summary
Psalm 145:18	
Matthew 5:44-45a	
James 1:5	
Philippians 2:3-4	

Now we are going to move on to my very favorite lesson from Hagar's life. It's a personal one for me, and I may end up crying before I finish all my thoughts. As a matter of fact, I'm going to grab some tissues right now before I start typing.

Okay. I'm ready.

To rehash: Sarai is mad, Abram is weak-willed, Hagar is mistreated, and she runs away. An angel of the LORD appears to Hagar, pronounces a blessing concerning her unborn son, and tells her to return to Sarai.

Here's where my tears start flowing.

> *She gave this name to the Lord who spoke to her: "You are the God who sees me," for she said, "I have now seen the One who sees me" (Genesis 16:13).*

Friends, Hagar was a slave girl. In the eyes of the world, she had little to no value. She had been mistreated and used. She was alone and scared. But our God saw her. He had compassion and deep, deep love for her. This means so much to the lonely woman that she gives Him a name.

El Roi. The words in Hebrew mean "The God who sees."[3]

I first learned of this name in 2003 when I was in a women's Bible study group in Albuquerque, New Mexico. We were studying the names of God. I was pregnant with my second child, and my husband had just been deployed to Iraq for Operation Iraqi Freedom.

I was a hot mess. Ladies, I mean it. I have never been so afraid in my life. Every knock at the door and every phone call made my heart stop. I loved Jesus, but I was gripped by fear. It didn't help that the 24-hour news cycle covered nothing but the war. All I knew was that the 1st Marine Division was heading to Baghdad…and that my husband was a part of it. *Would I ever see him again?*

Then one day I made it through enough of one of the Bible study lessons to learn about Hagar and the precious name she gave God. *El Roi*. When I couldn't sleep, when I thought about raising my children alone, when I prayed to keep it together for my toddler and my unborn son…God saw me.

When I couldn't eat, when I ate too much, when I couldn't stop watching CNN, when I was choking with worry…*El Roi* was near.

Sweet sisters…

Have you ever felt unimportant?
Have you ever been utterly helpless and alone?
Have you ever wondered how you would make it through?

I am here to tell you…God sees you. Scripture is crying out…*El Roi* is with you and will never leave you.

Scripture is crying out… El Roi is with you and will never leave you.

You are not alone.

And it's not just that God sees you. He is a God of action!

Psalm 46:1 tells us:

> *God is our refuge and strength,*
> *always ready to help in times of trouble.*

Look up **Matthew 11:28** and fill in the blanks:

> *Then Jesus said, "Come to me, all of you who are ___________ and carry heavy burdens, and I will give you_________."*

Looking back on that time of my life when fear had me by the throat, my God saw me. He gave me strength. He gave me rest. He comforted me and reminded me that He is enough. *El Roi*. To this day, that name brings tears to my eyes.

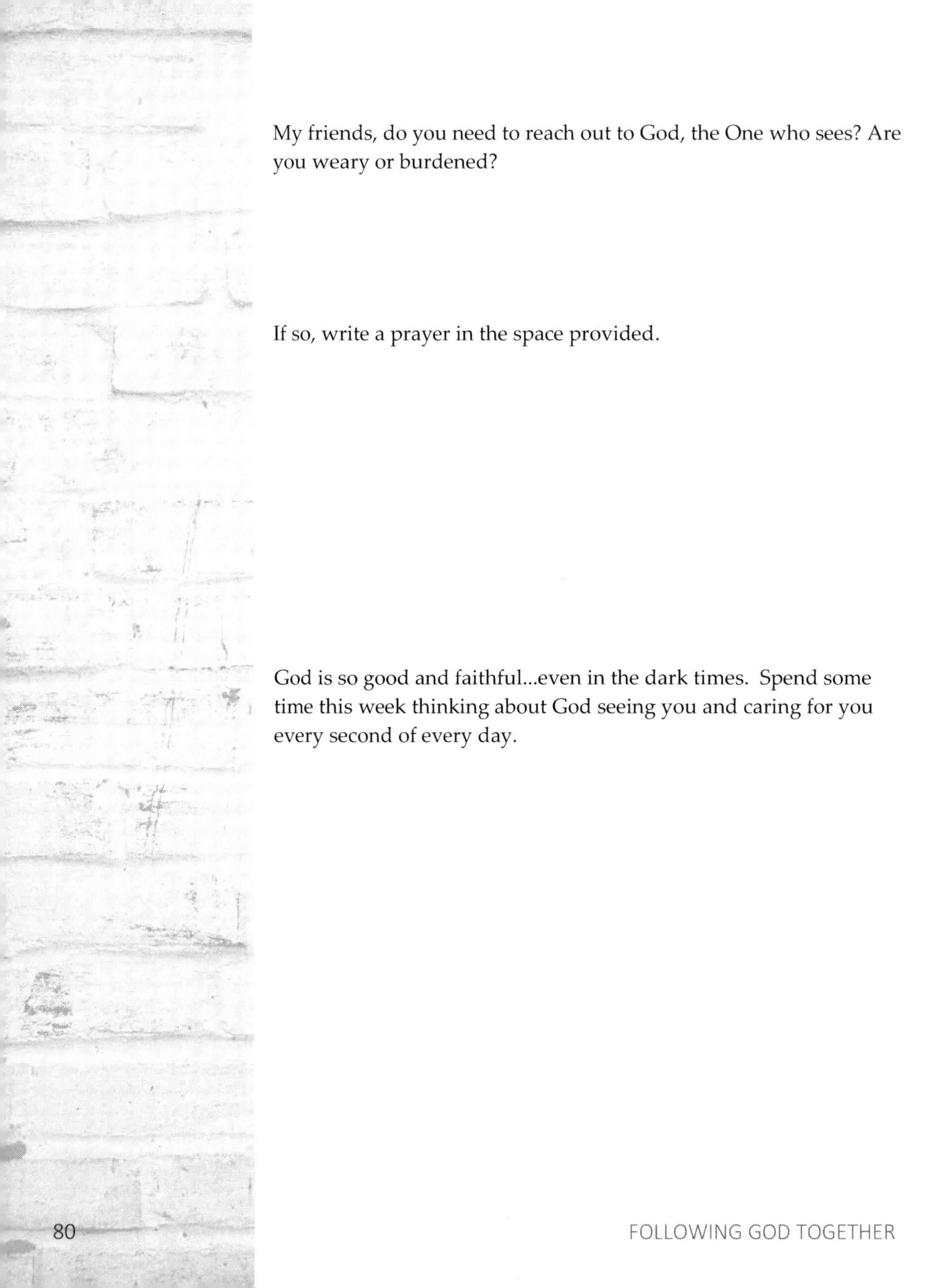

My friends, do you need to reach out to God, the One who sees? Are you weary or burdened?

If so, write a prayer in the space provided.

God is so good and faithful...even in the dark times. Spend some time this week thinking about God seeing you and caring for you every second of every day.

Day 3

PROMISES MADE, PROMISES KEPT

In this week's homework assignments, it may seem like I have thrown Sarai and Hagar under the bus. And in a way, I have. We spent a lot of our time learning from the *error of their ways*. God wants us to learn from His Word, from the people in Scripture. If all I ever read was, "These people were great. They always did what God asked"…I would never be able to relate!

That's our God! He takes broken people like you and me and fulfills His purpose for His glory.

Remember this verse from Day 1?

> *All Scripture is inspired by God and is useful to teach us what is true and to make us realize what is wrong in our lives. It corrects us when we are wrong and teaches us to do what is right. God uses it to prepare and equip his people to do every good work (2 Timothy 3:16-17).*

Now that's what I'm talking about. ALL SCRIPTURE. We get to see people mess up and then be forgiven. Restored then given purpose. That's our God! He takes broken people like you and me and fulfills His purpose for His glory. Beautiful, isn't it?

Which phrase from the verse above speaks to you? Why?

In today's study, we are going to look at the faithfulness of God. He blessed both Sarai and Hagar, two people who didn't get along and made questionable decisions. God made promises to all three of the key people in this story, and He was going to fulfill them.

READ Genesis 15:4-5.

Who is God speaking with and what did He promise?

Abram, Sarai's husband, was promised a son. Sarai got tired of waiting, and we all know what happened. But God loved Hagar, too. El Roi, the God who sees, comforted Hagar and made her a promise of huge proportion.

As a refresher, look up what God promised to Hagar in Genesis 16:10. How many descendants will she have?

And now for Sarai's promise. **READ** Genesis 17:15-16 then fill in the blanks with the words from verse 16.

Then God said to Abraham, "Regarding Sarai, your _____________—her name will no longer be Sarai. From now on her name will be Sarah. And I will bless her and give you a _____________ from her! Yes, I will bless her richly, and she will become the mother of many nations. Kings of nations will be among her descendants."

Wow! Now that's a promise! And I have to laugh just a little. This time God was very clear…"You're having a baby with Sarai, Abram. Sarai."

Did you note that Sarai is now Sarah? God also changed Abram's name to Abraham. I'll use their new names from here on out.

Abraham, Sarah, and Hagar have all been promised more descendants than they can count. But there is still trouble brewing within this family unit.

What's in a name?

Abram means "exalted father" while Abraham means "father of many."

Sarai and Sarah both mean the same thing…princess.

Abraham's name change seems to make sense. But why did God change Sarai to Sarah if they both have the same meaning?

The renaming stressed that she was to be the mother of nations and kings and thus to serve the Lord's purpose.[4]

Let's put together a list of what's happening in Genesis 21.

Verses 2-3: Sarah has a son for Abraham. They name him Isaac.
Verse 5: Abraham was ________ years old.
Verse 8: Isaac is about to be weaned, so Abraham is putting together a celebration for him.
Verse 9: "But Sarah saw Ishmael-the son of Abraham and her Egyptian servant Hagar ________________________ ____."
Verse 10: Sarah is furious and demands that Abraham send Hagar and Ishmael away.
Verses 11-14: Abraham is upset, but God consoles him. God tells him to do what Sarah asks, but that he will also make a nation out of Ishmael.
Verses 15-18: Hagar and Ishmael leave. They wander in the wilderness and get really thirsty. Hagar believes that Ishmael will die. An angel appears to her and reassures her of God's promise.
Verse 19: "Then God opened________________, and she saw a ____________________________."
Verse 20: God was with Ishmael as he grew, Ishmael became an archer, and they settled in Paran. His mother arranged for him to marry a woman from Egypt.

Did your ears perk up when you filled in the blank for verse 9? Mine sure did! Ooooooo, sis. There is nothing like a mama when her baby is being picked on or bullied! Sarah had had it!

Have you ever felt like Sarah? Have you ever "had enough" of a relationship? List a few details in the margin and then pray for God to give you peace if He hasn't already. In other words, hand your heart and emotions over to Him. He can handle it.

The Bible is full of families with turmoil and strife. Read through the following to get a taste of the drama.

In Genesis 27, two brothers fight over their father's blessing.

In Genesis 29, a father tricks Jacob into marrying the "other" sister. He ends up marrying both women.

And in Genesis 30, not surprisingly, these sisters are mad and jealous.

Goodness. Families are tough.

And Abraham's family is no different. As far as we know, Hagar never again meets up with Sarah and Abraham. Scripture never puts the trio together after Genesis 21. The relationship is over.

I don't know about you, but I don't have to go far down my family tree to find a fractured, never-mended relationship. To this day, I only know a few details of a split that happened before I was born. But I do know this, it was hard. Excruciatingly painful.

Following God doesn't mean that life always comes easy, we are immune to problems, or our relationships will always last. People are people, after all, and we are all broken.

If you are dealing with the effects of a severed relationship, I am so sorry. But more than that, my precious friend, God sees you. And He has promises for you.

READ the verse in the margin and then rewrite it below in your own words.

And we know that God causes everything to work together for the good of those who love God and are called according to his purpose for them.

ROMANS 8:28

Romans 8:28 has meant a lot to me over the years. I always keep in mind that not all things that happen are good, but that God makes good come out of anything for those who love Him. I am praying that for you and for me…and God can be trusted to do what He says!

> *God will do this, for he is faithful to do what he says, and he has invited you into partnership with his Son, Jesus Christ our Lord (1 Corinthians 1:9).*

Underline the second phrase. Now circle it. And finally draw a star above it. It's that important to remember this! It is high time that as Christ-followers, we make up our minds. Do we believe in God? If so, then we must BELIEVE Him, too.

The following verses contain promises of God. Circle one or two that you would like to grab onto…believing Him to be faithful.

> *You will keep in perfect peace all who trust in you, all whose thoughts are fixed on you! (Isaiah 26:3).*

> *And this same God who takes care of me will supply all your needs from his glorious riches, which have been given to us in Christ Jesus (Philippians 4:19).*

> *For I know the plans I have for you," says the Lord. "They are plans for good and not for disaster, to give you a future and a hope" (Jeremiah 29:11).*

> *So let's not get tired of doing what is good. At just the right time we will reap a harvest of blessing if we don't give up (Galatians 6:9).*

> *The temptations in your life are no different from what others experience. And God is faithful. He will not allow the temptation to be more than you can stand. When you are tempted, he will show you a way out so that you can endure (1 Corinthians 10:13).*

Do we believe in God? If so, then we must BELIEVE Him, too.

The Lord is close to the brokenhearted; he rescues those whose spirits are crushed (Psalm 34:18).

I could keep going and going with verses on God's promises and all He has for His people. He loves us with an everlasting love! It is impossible for God to forget us. He has good plans for us. We are His children.

The story of Abraham, Sarah, and Hagar is a difficult one, but God uses these sometimes faithful, sometimes rebellious people to tell His story to the world. Abraham is the founder of the Jewish nation. Sarah is listed in the Hall of Faith in Hebrews 11 and is an ancestor of Jesus.[5] Hagar's descendants are indeed too numerous to count.

Amazing, isn't it?

Before we end today's homework, let's take one last look at Ishmael and Isaac.

READ Genesis 25:7-9.

The two brothers, torn apart by family dysfunction, reunite for this solemn occasion to pay honor to their father. But for the rest of their days, the brothers lived at odds with each other.

My dear sisters, sometimes relationships don't work out the way we would like or even pray for. But remember, God isn't finished. He is working all things out for those who love Him and are called according to His purposes.

All things work for good. A promise is a promise.

Friendship Lesson:

A true friend delights in you.

Live It Out:

How are you going to apply what you've learned this week to your own life?

Prayer:

Heavenly Father, thank you for your honest and trustworthy guidance. Please be with me as I learn from other's mistakes and from my own mistakes. Help me to see people through your eyes. In the mighty name of Jesus. Amen.

Session 4: "Sarai & Hagar" Video Notes

Friendship Builder Questions

Do NOT feel the need to go in order or fit all the questions into the time allotted. Each woman should choose at least one of the questions to ask in her small group. Then get to talking and sharing your hearts with each other!

1. Why is it so hard to be vulnerable?
2. Have you ever become friends with someone you didn't connect with at first?
3. Have you ever had a frenemy?
4. Who do you relate more to, Sarai or Hagar? Why?
5. Do you lean towards thinking the best or worst of people you've just met?
6. Has God ever shown up for you when you were all alone?
7. What is the best compliment you've ever received?
8. Who do you wish you could get back in contact with?
9. Would you prefer to live in the same city as your extended family or out-of-state? (You have permission to skip this question if you have family members in your group with you. Lol!)
10. Share a promise God has made and kept with you.

Prayer Requests:

Week Five

PAUL & BARNABAS

Paul and Barnabas were friends, ministry partners, and integral to the growth of the early church. Their relationship had some ups and downs, like many of ours do, but it's amazing to see how God used their partnership so powerfully.

If you've ever found yourself in a friendship that ran into some disagreements…and let's be honest, who hasn't? I think you will find new purpose in this week's lesson. Of course, not all conflict is healthy, but neither can we say that it is always unhealthy. God can use these challenging situations for our growth or to produce something that might not have occurred without it.

I want God to use all of the relationships in my life to draw me closer to him. This includes friendships that seem to fly by conflict-free and those that challenge me more.

- **Day 1: Take a Chance**
  Be someone's Barnabas!
- **Day 2: Be Intentional**
  Every relationship needs attention to grow.
- **Day 3: Breaking Up is Hard to Do**
  God can bring good out of brokenness.

Day 1

TAKE A CHANCE

First, let's get to know Barnabas. For instance, his real name wasn't even Barnabas. It was actually Joseph; he was nicknamed Barnabas because it means what?

READ Acts 4:32-37.

- ❑ Son of Thunder
- ❑ Son of Joseph
- ❑ Son of Encouragement
- ❑ Son of Patience

All the believers were united in heart and mind. And they felt that what they owned was not their own, so they shared everything they had.

ACTS 4:32

What self-less thing did Barnabas do as a new believer?

A big part of me wishes I could have been one of those new believers seeing everyone on fire with their faith. Brothers and sisters willing to put aside all claim to material wealth for the good of the community and the spread of the Gospel. How exciting those days must have been to experience! Of course, there is the other side of me...the one that likes owning my own home!

What would you have a hard time giving up?

READ Acts 11:19-24.

When the church in Jerusalem heard about Gentiles in Antioch coming to the Lord in large numbers, they sent Barnabas to check it out. What did Barnabas conclude?

Depending on your translation, you may have read words like grace of God, joy, rejoiced, or encouraged. Barnabas was chosen for this mission because he *"was a good man, full of the Holy Spirit and strong in faith. And many people were brought to the Lord"* (Acts 11:24). I truly hope people would be able to say the same about us!

Now let's turn our thoughts towards Paul. Did you know he also went by two names? Saul was his Hebrew name and the name he would have been called in his Jewish community. Paul is the Latinized version of Saul, which would have been considered his Roman name. As he moved into his primary calling of being a missionary to the Gentiles, he became better known by his Gentile name, Paul. [1]

Saul is first mentioned in Acts 7:57 – 8:1 that describes the stoning of Stephen, a man full of faith and the Holy Spirit.

> *"His [Stephen's] accusers took off their coats and laid them at the feet of a young man named Saul…Saul was one of the witnesses, and he agreed completely with the killing of Stephen."*

The depth of hatred Saul had for Christians is revealed in Acts 9:1.

> *"Meanwhile, Saul was uttering threats with every breath and was eager to kill the Lord's followers."*

Friends, we are never a lost cause with God!

Wow! This guy "agreed completely with the killing," was "uttering threats," and was "eager to kill." Honestly, I probably would have written this man off as a lost cause. But God looks at him and says…this is one I can use. Friends, we are *never* a lost cause with God! Hallelujah!

Saul then had a come-to-Jesus moment (literally) on the road to Damascus in Acts 9. The pendulum swung and Saul began preaching about Jesus with the same level of intensity and focus he had used to persecute believers only days before.

I love it when God takes our plan and turns it on its head! He is so full of surprises!

I love it when God takes our plan and turns it on its head! He is so full of surprises!

I have experienced God's redirection many times. For instance, I always had this feeling I would one day adopt a child. My plan was to have a few babies first, then, once I was a "good" parent, welcome in a child who needed a home. However, God's plan (and the reason he had given me a heart for adoption in the first place), was because He would ask me to adopt a toddler from within my own extended family. She would be my oldest and have special needs. I had not imagined this in "my" plan, but God's plans are always better and I wouldn't change them for anything.

Can you think of a time in your life when you had a plan but God sent you in an unexpected direction?

READ Acts 9:22-28.

Saul is run out of Damascus for preaching too powerfully and proving the case of Jesus as the Messiah a little too well. He decides to head over to Jerusalem to meet with the believers there. Not without reason, they were all afraid of him. "They did not believe he had truly become a believer!" (Acts 9:26).

Have you ever doubted someone's conversion to Christ? Or witnessed someone's life make a 180 degree turn when they gave their life to Christ? Describe it briefly.

Who was willing to take a chance on believing Saul? (Acts 9:27)

Yes, you got it, the Son of Encouragement...because his nickname was an accurate depiction of his character. I can only guess how encouraged Saul was after hearing Barnabas testify to the apostles of how the Lord was using this persecutor turned evangelist.

God bless the Barnabases of this world! Have you ever had someone who was willing to put his or her name on the line for you? Describe who and how they blessed you. Thank God for the gift of them!

Day 2 BE INTENTIONAL

Let's start today by getting into God's Word. **READ** Acts 13:1-13.

Friends, this is a big deal! The first recorded missionary duo was sent out into the world.

Who went with Paul and Barnabas as their assistant (Acts 13:5)?

Who left their ministry (Acts 13:13)?

John Mark plays a significant role in Paul and Barnabas' relationship. He starts the missionary journey with them, with the intent to go the distance, and yet doesn't. Soon we will look at why this created a ripple effect in all of their lives.

Once John Mark left, Paul and Barnabas continued to visit town after town, offering Jews the opportunity to recognize Jesus as the Messiah prophesied in Scripture. The Messiah destined to come and rescue them. Unfortunately, many couldn't change the image they expected of a powerful political leader to match the truth of who Jesus actually was, a humble Savior. This realization led Paul and Barnabas to make a bold declaration that is still reverberating today and is the reason many of us have had the opportunity to know Jesus.

READ Acts 13:46 – 47.

What announcement did they make which opened the door for you and me?

Gentiles are non-Jews. Jews make up less than .2% of the world's population, which means the other 99.8% of people fall into the Gentile category.[2]

I've been guilty of thinking Paul alone opened the door to preaching Jesus to Gentiles, but after studying this relationship, I realized I inadvertently removed Barnabas from the narrative. Throughout their missionary journey, both men are listed time and time again as they spoke out boldly about Jesus.

READ the following verses and list in the margin if you see any patterns.

Pattern One	Pattern Two
Acts 12:25	Acts 13:16
Acts 13:1-4	Acts 14:19-20
Acts 13:7-8	Acts 15:35-36

PATTERN ONE:

PATTERN TWO:

In Pattern one, Barnabas' name is said first when mentioning the pair. In Pattern two, we see a switch and Paul's name is listed first from then forward. Many scholars believe that the order of their names signifies that Barnabas was the leader in their ministry until Paul started preaching to the Gentiles (see Acts 13:16). This becomes their main mission and Paul then takes the lead role.[3]

READ Acts 13:48-52, taking special note of verse 50. Who did the Jews "stir up" or "incite?"

Depending on your translation, the women mentioned may have been described as God-fearing, religious, worshipping, devout, prominent, honored, or important. Unfortunately, these women allowed themselves to be manipulated into using their influence for evil. From the wisdom of Spiderman, "With great power comes great responsibility." Friends, we must be careful who we allow to influence us and how we use our influence.

Can you think of a time when a group of women in your life used their influence in a harmful way? Describe it briefly.

We must be careful who we allow to influence us and how we use our influence.

How about when women used their influence in a godly way? How did they?

How do you think God wants you to use your influence?

Paul and Barnabas continued in their ministry throughout the region, experiencing both the peaks and valleys with each other. The excitement of seeing many people come to know Jesus as Lord, but also enduring severe persecution. Not your everyday kind of persecution either, we are talking about being beaten with rods, stoned and Paul being left for dead at one point.[4] I imagine Paul and Barnabas developed a deep bond quickly, especially as they faced a myriad of extreme experiences.Although I pray we never have to experience life or death situations to bond us, we do know what it is like to live day in and day out with others.

Take a trip down memory lane with me…Did you live in a dorm as a new freshman or ever go to a summer camp when you were a teenager? It's common to start out as acquaintances or even strangers in the beginning, but somewhere along the way, as you travel together, eat together, and bunk together…a bond quickly develops. Every great friendship started out as strangers in the beginning!

Have you had friends that walked alongside you, rejoicing in your greatest moments and carrying you through your deepest challenges? If so, list their names below.

Every great friendship started out as strangers in the beginning!

Whether you've experienced this or not, what do you think is the benefit of having friends like that?

As Christians, we are recipients of many benefits, not the least of which is that Jesus wants to be our friend. We have no secrets with Jesus, even if we try to hide something from Him, it's just not possible. He is right there with us rejoicing in the peaks and carrying us through the valleys. He knows the deepest darkest secret you've told no one else… and He loves you more than you can ever imagine.

> *No longer do I call you servants, for the servant does not know what his master is doing; but I have called you friends, for all that I have heard from my Father I have made known to you (John 15:15, ESV).*

Do you consider Jesus your friend? Why or why not?

It's difficult to have a deep friendship with someone if you don't spend time with them. Every relationship needs attention to grow. With this in mind, here are some ideas below to help you deepen your friendship with Jesus.

It's difficult to have a deep friendship with someone if you don't spend time with them.

- Do a 30-day challenge to only listen to Christian music.
- Commit to reading your Bible for ____ minutes a day.
- Listen to the Bible using a phone app.
- Spend more time in prayer, either on your own or with a friend.

Be intentional about your relationship with Jesus and others and watch God bless your efforts!

Day 3

BREAKING UP IS HARD TO DO

One of my teenage daughters went through a "friend break-up." The two girls met the first day of middle school and were fast friends. Sharing everything. Laughing constantly. It was one of those rare friendships I thought would last the test of time. However, after over two years of this closeness, their worldviews clashed in a heated disagreement. Even though my daughter was okay with their differences, it turned out the other girl's family wasn't and their relationship was abruptly severed. My daughter mourned the loss of this friendship. It was a difficult season for her, bringing a feeling of hopelessness to her door.

Have you ever experienced a "friend break-up?" Describe it briefly.

Paul and Barnabas also experienced a "friend break-up." Even though Paul and Barnabas worked alongside each other and enjoyed great fellowship, it didn't mean they agreed on everything.

After completing their first missionary journey, they ended up back in Antioch of Syria.

READ Acts 15:36-41.

Paul wanted to go back to visit all of the believers. He realized this was not a one-and-done missionary trip. His heart yearned to go back and check on his new brothers and sisters. Keep in mind…this is before cell phones and social media. If he wanted to know how they were doing, he would need to put on his walking sandals and get ready for some dusty feet.

Who did Barnabas want to bring with them on their return trip?

He's back! Or at least *Barnabas* wants him back on the team. In our previous lesson this week, we learned that John Mark left Paul and Barnabas early on during their first missionary journey with no clear indication of why. Yet, in Acts 15:38 we clearly see Paul felt he had deserted them.

Have you had any friends who have deserted or abandoned you? How did you feel about them afterwards? Were you able to make amends or did it end the friendship?

Paul and Barnabas end up having an intense argument and heading off in different directions. Paul teams up with Silas while Barnabas pairs off with John Mark.

Brainstorm: What good came out of this conflict?

You may have noticed that the ministry was doubled. Instead of two men heading off in one direction, there were now four men with the potential to reach twice as many people.

Even if Satan rejoiced over this division, God meant to bring about multiplication. It reminds me of what Joseph said to his brothers when they were worried he would retaliate against them now that he was in a position of power.

> *"You intended to harm me, but God intended it all for good. He brought me to this position so I could save the lives of many people" (Genesis 50:20).*

Think about your example of a conflict with a friend, whether it was a friend break-up or a desertion. Can you think of **any** good that came out of it?

If you can't see anything, it's never too late. Take a moment and pray, asking God to bring something good out of it for you. Maybe God will put someone in your path who has experienced something similar and needs an empathetic ear and understanding heart; that, my friend, could be you!

Let's take a walk through Scripture and discover more about John Mark. Look up each verse and write what it tells you.

READ the verses in the margins and fill in the correct names.

Acts 12:12-13
John Mark was the son of ____________ , whose home was a meeting place for believers.

Colossians 4:10
Mark was the cousin of __________________ , yes...you read that right.

We can extrapolate a few things from this information. For one, Acts 12:12-13 tells us that John Mark's family had a home big enough to host meetings for believers, and a servant, Rhoda, so it isn't too big of a jump to assume his family was financially well-off.

When he realized this, he went to the home of Mary, the mother of John Mark, where many were gathered for prayer. He knocked at the door in the gate, and a servant girl named Rhoda came to open it.

ACTS 12:12-13

Aristarchus, who is in prison with me, sends you his greetings, and so does Mark, Barnabas's cousin. As you were instructed before, make Mark welcome if he comes your way.

COLOSSIANS 4:10

We aren't told why John Mark left during the first missionary trip but for all we know he could have been pressured by family to go, or not ready for the intense level of persecution they would face, or maybe he was just plain homesick. What we do know is he wanted to try again.

Barnabas, true to character, decided he was willing to put his reputation on the line for his cousin, John Mark, just as he had done for Saul. He believed this time around, John Mark would make it.

Do you think people change? YES or NO

What can inspire lasting change in someone?

Do you have any examples you can share?

Where are you on your spiritual evolution?
Place an "x" somewhere along the continuum.

Beginner ———————————————— Pro

If we believe we can change, then it is possible for others to as well.

Do you hope to move up the scale? YES or NO

What will you have to change to do so?

If we believe we can change, then it is possible for others to change as well. My prayer is to always be growing and transforming to become more like Jesus. As Christians, we have the amazing benefit of knowing God wants to help us.

> *Don't copy the behavior and customs of this world, but* ***let God transform you into a new person by changing the way you think****. Then you will learn to know God's will for you, which is good and pleasing and perfect. (Romans 12:2, emphasis mine).*

John Mark's transformation was validated when he later became the Apostle Peter's assistant. Although all of the Gospels are written anonymously, it is widely believed that John Mark wrote the book of Mark based on Peter's eyewitness accounts.[5]

The best part of the story comes in the reconciliation.

Look up these verses, all written by Paul, and note what they tell us about John Mark:

Colossians 4:10

Philemon 23-24

2 Timothy 4:11

There is no mention in the Bible of Barnabas after he and Paul head off in different ministry directions, but there is something in the book of Luke that hints at a heart change. Let's go back to a verse we looked at on our first day of study this week.

> *"Barnabas was a good man, full of the Holy Spirit and strong in faith. And many people were brought to the Lord" (Acts 11:24).*

We may not know if they ever saw each other again, but "Luke wrote this description of Barnabas after the confrontation between Paul and Barnabas…since Luke was Paul's traveling companion, this statement about Barnabas must have been Paul's assessment as well."[6]

One disagreement didn't prevent Paul from seeing all the good in Barnabas. I can only imagine Barnabas' joy, whether it was here or in heaven, to hear that Paul and John Mark were woven together once again.

Just as Paul and John Mark were reunited, God wants our relationship with Him to be reconciled, too. Spend some time today meditating on this verse:

> *For God in all his fullness was pleased to live in Christ,*
> *and through him God reconciled everything to himself.*
> *He made peace with everything in heaven and on earth*
> *by means of Christ's blood on the cross (Colossians 1:19-20).*

Friendship Lesson:

Conflict can be used for our good.

Live It Out:

How are you going to apply what you've learned this week to your own life?

Prayer:

Dear Heavenly Father, thank you for the example of Paul and Barnabas. Help me to remember that healthy conflicts can produce good and necessary changes in my life. Give me a heart for reconciliation and give me eyes to see how you will bring good out of every friendship challenge. Amen.

Session 5: "Paul & Barnabas" Video Notes

Friendship Builder Questions

Do NOT feel the need to go in order or fit all the questions into the time allotted. Each woman should choose at least one of the questions to ask in her small group. Then get to talking and sharing your hearts with each other!

1. Have you ever gone on a mission trip? What was your biggest take-away?
2. What is something that people often misunderstand about you?
3. What were the biggest instigators of growth and change in your life?
4. Would you rather face conflict or avoid it?
5. Have you ever had a serious disagreement with a friend and been able to resolve it? Share a few details.
6. What is a deal-breaker in your friendships?
7. What are your three biggest pet peeves?
8. What is one thing you got rejected for that ended up being a blessing in disguise?
9. Have you ever had a friend betray you?
10. What's your favorite verse?

Prayer Requests:

Week Six

MARY AND MARTHA

Just imagine it. Jesus loves coming to your home to rest, eat, and enjoy your company. The long awaited Messiah teaches in your living room, walks through your kitchen, and calls you by name. When Jesus passes through town, it is with you He wants to stay. Your hospitality becomes legendary…literally. Your name is penned into God's Holy Word as the preferred bed and breakfast of the Son of God!

But it sure does take some work to prepare for a house filled with guests…because we know Jesus never traveled alone! There are meals to prepare, beds to make, and floors to sweep. If only you could get your sister to help…

Welcome to the story of Mary and Martha. Two sisters who share a home and call Jesus a friend. There are plenty of lessons to learn this week, so let's dive in.

- **Day 1: Where's Your Focus?**
  Spending time with God changes everything.

- **Day 2: Different Gifts, Same God**
  Accepting your gifts and the differences in others brings peace and joy.

- **Day 3: You're Welcome**
  Hospitality is a matter of the heart.

Day 1

WHERE'S YOUR FOCUS?

I have always been captivated by the story of Mary and Martha. I also have a brother and sister I love very much, even though we have very different personalities. However, I am mostly drawn to this story because I can relate to both Mary and Martha. Like Mary, I truly enjoy having people in my home and around my table, and like Martha, I jump for joy when I can mark something off my to-do list. And like both of them, I love Jesus.

Let's get started by reading their story in Luke 10:38-42.

I can just imagine the conversation between the two sisters.

"Mary! He's almost here! Come and help me in the kitchen. Can you cut the vegetables? Oh, no! I think we're out of olive oil. Can you run over to the neighbor's to get some? The floor! It's a mess! Get the broom!"

"Martha. Relax. It's Jesus! He doesn't care about our floors. Can't we just visit with Him when He gets here?"

One sister wanted everything just so, while the other thought, "C'mon…those things aren't important!"

Poor Martha. Doing all the work and becoming more frustrated by the second. And sweet Mary. Getting fussed at for hanging out with God's Son. Spending time with Jesus is one of my favorite things, but sometimes my family wants to eat dinner, too!

To get started on our quest, answer this question: How did Jesus respond to Martha and her request of Him?

But the Lord said to her, "My dear Martha, you are worried and upset over all these details! There is only one thing worth being concerned about. Mary has discovered it, and it will not be taken away from her."

LUKE 10:41-42

Ouch. That must've stung a little. Martha was not expecting Jesus to side with her sister!

If you were Martha in the story, what might you have thought after Jesus' response? Mark as many as you want.

- ❑ But I need help!
- ❑ That isn't fair.
- ❑ Why does she get out of work?
- ❑ Why am I the one who gets stuck in the kitchen?
- ❑ But if I sit at your feet, who will finish dinner?
- ❑ Other: ______________________________________

Look up this short verse and write it out.

Philippians 2:14.

Most of us are able to do *some* things without complaint. The difficulty arises when we are asked to do "everything" with a joyful spirit. Yet that is what we are called to do.[1]

What things do you struggle doing without complaint?

Did putting away laundry make your list? It's on mine. I don't so much mind the washing and drying…it's just actually putting it away!

For all the Marthas out there, you may be feeling a little devalued right about now. Please don't feel that way! Look again at verse 41. Did you notice the phrase, "My dear Martha…" Isn't Jesus kind and gentle? He wasn't scolding the older sister for serving, but he needed her to learn something very important.

Write your name in the blank and imagine Jesus saying this to you:
My dear ______________________________.

No shame. No condemnation. Kindness and love.

So now there is no condemnation for those who belong to Christ Jesus.

ROMANS 8:1

And please know this…the world needs Marthas!

READ Acts 6:1-4 for confirmation:

> *But as the believers rapidly multiplied, there were rumblings of discontent. The Greek-speaking believers complained about the Hebrew-speaking believers, saying that their widows were being discriminated against in the daily distribution of food.*
>
> *So the Twelve called a meeting of all the believers. They said, "We apostles should spend our time teaching the word of God, not running a food program. And so, brothers, select seven men who are well respected and are full of the Spirit and wisdom. We will give them this responsibility. Then we apostles can spend our time in prayer and teaching the word."*

Did you pick up on it? The apostles wanted to pray and teach (Mary), but they also needed people to take care of the physical needs of others (Martha). There's room for Mary and Martha in the family of believers!

This is where God gets to the heart of the matter. In Acts 6, what were the Apostles looking for in the seven responsible men who were to feed the hungry?

The men chosen for this very important task had to be full of God above all else! That's the key for each and every one of us.

Which brings us back to Mary, sitting at the feet of Jesus.

"There is only one thing worth being concerned about. Mary has discovered it, and it will not be taken away from her" (Luke 10:42).

What is that one thing?

Spending time with Jesus. Being close to God. Knowing Him, choosing Him, being friends with Him. God makes Himself perfectly clear; He wants your heart *before* He wants your service.

But this is also where I hear you saying, "What about all the things I have to do? Seriously. I have to work."

God understands that we have things to do. He knows the responsibilities we carry. God gave the Apostle Paul a huge mission. He was to spread the Gospel to the Gentiles. Paul traversed all over the Mediterranean planting churches, preaching God's Word, arguing with religious leaders, and writing letters that make up the majority of the New Testament. He didn't have time to always sit at the feet of Jesus!

READ 1 Thessalonians 5:16-18 and fill in the blanks with the words of Paul.

Always be joyful. ______________________________ . Be thankful ________________________________, for this is God's will for you ________________________________.

Possibly the busiest man of his time wrote "never stop praying." What? Never? How exactly do we do that?

Believe it or not, you can spend time with God in everything you do. By inviting Him to be a part of your daily activities, you stay aware of His presence.[2]

I don't want your sacrifices—
I want your love;
I don't want your offerings—
I want you to know me.

HOSEA 6:6

God makes Himself perfectly clear; He wants your heart ***before*** *He wants your service.*

Invite God into your everything. Talk to Him on your drive to work. Pray while washing dishes. Listen to worship music while walking or running. Bring Him into conversations with friends. Listen to or read the Bible. And yes…spend time alone with Him. Your heart will be like His in no time!

List some of the things you will do this week to get your heart closer to God. Be as specific as possible.

Example: Talk to him while I'm getting ready in the morning.

But the Holy Spirit produces this kind of fruit in our lives: love, joy, peace, patience, kindness, goodness, faithfulness, gentleness, and self-control. There is no law against these things!

GALATIANS 5:22-23

How do you think spending more time with God will improve your relationships? (Read the verse in the margin for ideas.)

Day 2

DIFFERENT GIFTS, SAME GOD

Today, let's continue with the relationship between the two sisters and their very dear friend. Open your Bible and **READ** John 12:1-3.

We are back at the home of Mary and Martha. This time, though, there's another member of the family present. Lazarus…Mary & Martha's brother.

What does verse 1 say about him?

Yes. You read that right. Jesus raised Lazarus from the dead, and Lazarus was sitting at the table eating with Jesus. (For more on that miraculous story, read John 11:1-44).

Let's zero in on our sisters.

What did Mary do and where do we find her?

Where is Martha in this story?

We find Mary at the feet of Jesus, and Martha is in the kitchen. Some things change. Some things stay the same.

Using today's passage and the one from Day 1 to list a few differences about the sisters. (Luke 10:38-42; John 12:1-3).

Mary	Martha

There are plenty of distinctions between the women. Martha is anxious. Mary is laid-back. Martha is Type A, while Mary is Type B. One is task-driven. The other is people-oriented.

Think of your own friends and family members. Everyone has his or her own way of doing things. My husband has his way of doing the dishes, and I have my way. My teenage daughter loves to run, while I've never enjoyed running a mile in my life. My friend enjoys staying up into the wee hours of the morning, and I struggle keeping my eyes open past eleven o'clock.

Differences between people make this world a lot more interesting, and it's by God's design! Look up Ephesians 2:10 and write it in the space below.

We are God's masterpiece. Think about that for a minute. Of all the wonderful and amazing things God created, He calls each one of us His pièce de résistance! You were created to do God's good works with what He gave you. The same goes for me.

Humbling isn't it? **READ** Romans 12:6-8 in the margin and answer a few questions.

Do you see something you're good at on the list? If so, what is it?

If not, list something else you're good at. (If you can't think of anything, ask God to reveal it to you…or ask a trusted friend.)

Now, let's think of people we know. I'm going to list out some different things from the passage, and I would like you to write down the name of someone you know who excels at that gift.

Serving others?

Encouraging people?

Giving generously?

Leading people?

Showing kindness?

Hearing from God?

The probability is good that you didn't write down the same name for every one of these. We are all good at something. But there isn't a single person on this planet who is good at everything. And that's just how God intended.

So here's the million-dollar question: If we are each God's masterpiece (which we are) and if God has given us different gifts to do certain things well (which He did), then why do we get so caught up in comparing ourselves to other people?

*In his grace, God has given us different gifts for doing certain things well. So if God has given you the ability to **prophesy**, speak out with as much faith as God has given you. If your gift is **serving** others, serve them well. If you are a **teacher**, teach well. If your gift is to **encourage** others, be encouraging. If it is **giving**, give generously. If God has given you **leadership** ability, take the responsibility seriously. And if you have a gift for showing **kindness** to others, do it gladly.*

ROMANS 12:6-8
(emphasis mine)

Let's make it a little more personal...

> Do you struggle comparing yourself to others? YES or NO
>
> Do you often see yourself as "less than" or "wanting more?" YES or NO
>
> Do you sometimes put others down to make yourself feel better? YES or NO

If you said yes to any or all of these questions, you are not alone. I struggle, too. I have a love/hate relationship with social media. I get on there to find a recipe or stay in touch with a long distance friend, and before I know it, my "once-content" heart has melted into a green pile of gelatinous envy.

All those beautiful photos of gorgeous backyard fire pits, exotic family vacations, and incredibly fabulous farmhouse weddings....oh why did I get married before the advent of Pinterest?!?!

Anyone with me? But this is not what God wants for me or you. Remember Ephesians 2:10...you are God's masterpiece. He has good works for you to do. And only you can do them!

READ Romans 12:6-8 again. You have a gift from God to do certain things well. Wouldn't it be a waste to miss out by wanting something else?

Remember Martha from our first day of homework? She was upset that her sister wasn't helping.

Now look back at today's passage, John 12:2-3.

> *A dinner was prepared in Jesus' honor. Martha served, and Lazarus was among those who ate with him. Then Mary took a twelve-ounce jar of expensive perfume made from essence of nard, and she*

anointed Jesus' feet with it, wiping his feet with her hair. The house was filled with the fragrance.

Do you notice anything different about Martha?

Something has changed. There is no mention of her fussing about Mary. Martha is serving while Mary is anointing Jesus. Two sisters, two different ways to serve and love Jesus. Could it be that Martha is now at peace with their different gifts? Is it possible that Jesus' gentle reproach from before…that God's Word…changed her?

My sweet friend…it's more than possible. Being in the presence of Jesus changes each and every one of us.

Before closing your book for the day, take a snapshot of James 1:25 or write it on a notecard. Do your best to put it into your heart this week. I'm praying as we go about God's business, He blesses us with His presence, peace, and joy.

But if you look carefully into the perfect law that sets you free, and if you do what it says and don't forget what you heard, then God will bless you for doing it.
James 1:25

Hospitality customs of the day called for a guest's feet to be washed when entering the home. This was an act of humility on Mary's part, because this act was usually done by a servant. Mary showed her devotion to Jesus not just by washing his feet, but by the extravagance of the perfume. Nard was very expensive and worth about a year's wages for a laborer.[3]

Day 3

YOU'RE WELCOME

My heart is full when I have a house full of people. I absolutely love life when there is food, friendship, and lots of laughter in my home and around my table. If you need easy dinner recipes, I'm your girl. Need help with table decor? I've got tons of ideas. I can turn an empty room into a festive atmosphere fit for a crowd in minutes. Hospitality is my happy place, and I am so grateful.

But is there more to hospitality than Instagram-worthy decorations and a charcuterie board?

The focus of entertaining is impressing people.

The focus of hospitality is serving others.[4]

As a matter of fact, yes! That's only a small piece of the puzzle. Today's lesson takes a look at hospitality and the many ways to extend the love of Jesus into the lives of others.

Let's start with the definition of hospitality.

> 1. *The friendly reception and treatment of guests or strangers.*
>
> 2. *The quality or disposition of receiving and treating guests and strangers in a warm, friendly, generous way.*[5]

We are going to start by thinking big. When have you been the recipient of warm, friendly, and generous hospitality? (Think church, friends, vacations, parties, etc.)

It probably felt really nice to be pampered, didn't it? The first time I was ever introduced to lavish hospitality was by my friend and mentor, Ivelisse Page. She and her husband were the leaders of a small group Bible study that my husband and I were attending.

Every Valentine's Day they would go "all out" for the couples in their group. They decorated their house, setup tables for two all over their home, and served a fancy three-course meal all while catering to our every need. Did I mention that most of us in that study were parents of very young children? You can imagine how much this special evening meant to a husband and wife who desperately needed to step away and reconnect.

Ivelisse was more than hospitable. She extended grace to exhausted parents. She created a moment that strengthened marriages. She exposed her own children (who helped serve dinner) to kindness and generosity. And she modeled the extravagant heart of Jesus to all of us in attendance.

Some of you may be thinking...*that sounds incredible! I'd love to be invited to something like that. But I don't think I have it in me to host that kind of event.* Before going down this thought path, I'd like to tell you that I don't recall looking into Ivelisse's bedrooms. I don't remember looking around for dust in the corners or dishes in the sink. I remember feeling grateful and blessed. People won't remember the meal you cooked, or the cleanliness of your house, but they will certainly remember how you made them feel.

Let's look up these verses and write down a few notes on each.

1 Peter 4:9

Romans 12:13

Keep these verses in mind as you read a definition of "biblical" hospitality.

If you've gotten anything at all out of following Christ, if his love has made any difference in your life, if being in a community of the Spirit means anything to you, if you have a heart, if you care—then do me a favor: Agree with each other, love each other, be deep-spirited friends. Don't push your way to the front; don't sweet-talk your way to the top. Put yourself aside, and help others get ahead. Don't be obsessed with getting your own advantage. Forget yourselves long enough to lend a helping hand.

PHILIPPIANS 2:3-4 (MSG)

"The welcoming and fellowshipping with believers and non-believers out of truth and love for Jesus Christ so that they may see Christ more clearly and/or so they will join us as exiles themselves (or join us as believers)."[6]

I just love this definition. It's so freeing! It's notable for all the words you don't find. Did you see the words "over the top" or "go to extreme lengths to clean your house so everyone will think well of you?" Nope. I didn't, either.

What does stand out to you about the biblical definition of hospitality?

From God's perspective, hospitality is about the heart. He wants us to welcome people into our lives so that He may be glorified. He wants His grace, love, warmth, and generosity extended to those already in the family of God and to those who have yet to believe.

From God's perspective, hospitality is about the heart. He wants us to welcome people into our lives so that He may be glorified.

With "easy yet purposeful" in mind, here is a list of possible ways to show hospitality to others. Place a check next to the ones you can do:

- ❑ Invite a friend over for coffee.
- ❑ Meet up with someone at a local restaurant or park.
- ❑ Go for a walk together.
- ❑ Zoom call a long-distance, lonely friend or relative.
- ❑ Invite a friend to a Bible study group or church service, then sit with them.
- ❑ Include someone in an activity you are already doing. (For instance…tasks, volunteer or neighborhood events, church activities, etc.)

I remember when my kids were little; it was easy to invite my friends and their children to meet us at the neighborhood pool or at the park. The littles could run around and play while we just had an adult conversation! Anything to get out of the house and do life together.

These friendship-building moments were also opportunities to see Christ more clearly.

- I would often hear Jesus' words spoken from a trusted confidante at just the right time.
- I would grab hold of the chance to lovingly speak God's truth into a new friend's situation.
- I would receive the simple, yet invaluable, gift of a friendship where Jesus is included.

Ask God to put one or two people on your heart who need a friendly invitation this week. Write down their names.

Now commit to asking them to meet up in the next few days.

Hospitality. Loving others well in the name of Jesus.

Mary learned this at the feet of her Savior and friend and then gave Him her heart. Martha learned this from Jesus' gentle correction and then joyfully served Him and others with her God-given gifts and talents.

We are all called to invite others into the audacious love of God. The world needs your gifts of compassion, love, and kindness.[7]

There are people in your neighborhood, your church, or your circle who need to be built up and encouraged by someone who knows and loves Jesus.

So get going! The God of the universe is calling you into relationship with Him and His people. Blessings, joy, and friendship await.

FRIENDSHIP BUILDING VERSES

As iron sharpens iron, so one person sharpens another.
PROVERBS 27:17

Quietly trust yourself to Christ your Lord, and if anybody asks why you believe as you do, be ready to tell him, and do it in a gentle and respectful way.
1 PETER 3:15

The heartfelt counsel of a friend is as sweet as perfume and incense.
PROVERBS 27:9

Friendship Lesson:

When your focus is on Jesus, relationships take priority; both with Him and with others.

Live it Out!

How are you going to apply what you've learned this week to your own life?

Prayer:

Heavenly Father, thank you for your Word that teaches me of your love. Please emblazon on my heart the gifts, talents, and abilities you have given me, make clear the good works you have for me to do, and free me from the trap of comparison. Help me to keep you as my first priority, recognizing the gifts in others and spurring them on in serving you. Change me to be more like you. In the mighty name of Jesus, Amen.

Session 6: "Mary & Martha" Video Notes

Do NOT feel the need to go in order or fit all the questions into the time allotted. Each woman should choose at least one of the questions to ask in her small group. Then get to talking and sharing your hearts with each other!

1. Given the choice of anyone in the world, whom would you want as a dinner guest?
2. Are you proud of what you're doing with your heart and time right now?
3. What's the best advice a family member gave you growing up?
4. What would you do if time weren't a concern?
5. What do you want to be remembered for?
6. Share a time a gentle rebuke helped you.
7. How many siblings do you have? Where are you in the birth order?
8. What's your go-to dish on a busy weeknight?
9. Do you lead with your heart or your head more often?
10. What activity or discipline centers your heart back on Jesus?

Prayer Requests:

Leader Guide

Our hearts are full of gratitude for each one of you ladies. Leading a group takes time, energy, commitment, and organization. But you can do it! And we want to help as much as we can with these tips.

Following God Together: Let's Talk About Friendship has been developed to help women grow deeper in their relationship with God and to encourage them to build more meaningful friendships.

Here is some information that will help you prepare and lead a successful and meaningful study.

SCHEDULE

- You will need 7 sessions to complete the study.
- There is one introductory video followed by 6 weekly videos that continue the lessons.
- Each individual session will require 90 minutes.

PROMOTE THE STUDY

- Get the word out about this study 4-6 weeks in advance.
- Emails, social media posts, calls or texts to potential members, and your church's website are great places to spread the word.
- A promotional video is available at www.entwinedministries.com.

BEFORE THE STUDY

- Pray for the women who will be attending…for God's protection, for their hearts to be open to hearing from Him, that the obstacles to their attendance will be removed, and for anything else God puts on your heart.
- Communicate with the women regarding dates, times, and location.
- Coordinate childcare for your members if necessary.
- Buy the necessary amount of workbooks or have each member buy their own.
- Purchase or download the videos from www.entwinedministries.com.
- Ensure that the video equipment is functioning properly.
- Have nametags, especially for the first few sessions.
- Designate a leader for each small group with no more than 8 women per group. This allows plenty of time for prayer, discussion, and getting to know each other.
- Keep track of "My Small Group Members" on page 131.

SESSION TIPS

- Create a warm and welcoming environment.
- Start and end on time.
- At the beginning of every session, go over the group guidelines listed on this page.
- Communicate with the women during the week to encourage them and build relationships.
- Pray for the study members during the week.
- Some women may find it difficult to share in groups. Try to encourage them as best you can to participate. Long silences are awkward, but sometimes necessary to allow quieter members time to think and share.
- Be ready to share first and model vulnerability when needed.
- If discussions get off topic, draw the conversation back to God's Word or the workbook question. Avoid opinions or trying to "fix" each other's problems.
- During the homework discussion time, go through day by day and ask the women if anything stood out to them or if they have questions. Be sure to discuss both topical and more personal questions.

SMALL GROUP AGENDA

- Welcome and sign-in (5 minutes)
- Opening prayer (2 minutes)
- Homework discussion (20 minutes)
- Video (20 minutes)
- Friendship Builder questions (25 minutes)
- Prayer requests and prayer (15 minutes)
- Closing thoughts and encouragement (3 minutes)

GROUP GUIDELINES

Share these as a reminder each week.

- **Be confidential.** Information shared should stay within the group.
- **Be concise.** Give everyone a chance to share.
- **Be prayerful.** Please share prayer requests after completing the Friendship Builder questions. Take the time to pray!
- **Be here.** You will get much more out of this study if you complete the homework lessons each week. However, we have a #NoShame policy here! We understand that things come up. Please attend the group even if you haven't done the homework. God will speak to you through the discussion, video, and group time.

MY SMALL GROUP MEMBERS

Name	Phone Number	Email	How do you prefer to be contacted?		
			Text	Call	Email
			☐	☐	☐
			☐	☐	☐
			☐	☐	☐
			☐	☐	☐
			☐	☐	☐
			☐	☐	☐
			☐	☐	☐
			☐	☐	☐
			☐	☐	☐
			☐	☐	☐
			☐	☐	☐
			☐	☐	☐
			☐	☐	☐
			☐	☐	☐
			☐	☐	☐
			☐	☐	☐

ACKNOWLEDGEMENTS

Over fifteen years ago, our dear friend and mentor, Francine Marshall, shared with us that God had given her a vision of the three of us having a future ministry together. That Word of the Lord never left the back of our minds, even when we moved to separate parts of the country. We all became involved in ministry in the places we were planted, but then just six months ago, God brought us back together and gave us a fresh vision of the plan He had for us. Entwined Ministries was born and this Bible study was laid on all of our hearts. It has been a whirlwind of a ride, but oh so exciting!

One of the first things God prompted us to do when we started this process was to gather a group of prayer warriors. They consistently brought us to the feet of Jesus and prayed us through this miraculous season. Thank you Candace, Christy, Francine, Jill, Kelly, Lindsey, and Shine.

And to the many who took the time to read through drafts and provide feedback…we truly appreciate you!

Our families have also fully supported us every step of the way. They encouraged us to keep going when we were tired, and made space for us to focus on what God was asking us to accomplish. Tim, Mitchell, Kyle, Lauren, Joe, Luke, Lindsey, Allie, Jerilyn, Ainsley and Daisy…you may be a list of names to everyone else, but to us, you are everything. We love you.

April Julie Maureen

ENDNOTES

WEEK 1

[1] New International Bible Commentary, Zondervan, 1999, page 1159.
[2] "Where the World Comes to Study the Bible." n.d., https://bible.org.
[3] Merriam-Webster Dictionary, "witness" January 22, 2021. https://www.merriam-webster.com.

WEEK 2

[1] Philip King and Lawrence Stager, *Life in Biblical Israel*, (Westminster John Knox Press, Louisville, 2001), p. 37.
[2] Dallas Theological Seminary, Roy B. Zuck and John Walvoord, *The Bible Knowledge Commentary*, (Scripture Press, 1985), p.205.
[3] Ibid., p.204.
[4] Maclaren, Alexander. 1900. *Expositions of Holy Scripture*. London, England: Hodder & Stoughton.
[5] Philippians 2:5-8.
[6] Dawn Wilson, "10 roles of the Holy Spirit in the Old Testament," July 1,2019, https://www.christianity.com/wiki/holy-spirit/10-roles-of-the-holy-spirit-in-the-old-testament.html
[7] Oxford English Dictionary, s.v. "mentor," February 9, 2021, www.google.com.
Fig.1 "From Nazareth to Judah," 2012, map, scale not given. "Explore the Life of Mary This Advent Season". Logos Blog. https://blog.logos.com/explore-the-life-of-mary-this-advent-season/

WEEK 3

[1] In 1 Samuel 18:3 most translations use the word covenant, although NLT uses the term solemn pact.
[2] "A Covenant of Friendship," The Pulpit Commentary. 2010. https://biblehub.com/sermons/auth/dale/a_covenant_of_friendship.htm
[3] NIV Cultural Backgrounds Study Bible. 2016. Grand Rapids, Michigan: Zondervan.
[4] Ibid, Douglas, Tenney and Silva.

WEEK 4

[1] NIV Cultural Backgrounds Study Bible. Copyright © 2016 by Zondervan.
[2] Tyndale. Essay. In *Holy Bible: Life Application Study Bible NLT*, 30–30. Carol Stream, IL: Tyndale House Publishers, 2016.
[3] Ibid, Douglas, Tenney and Silva.
[4] Barker, Kenneth L., and John R. Kohlenberger. Essay. In *The Expositor's Bible Commentary: Abridged Edition*. Grand Rapids, MI: Zondervan Pub. House, 1994.
[5] ibid

WEEK 5

[1] Henry, Matthew. Matthew Henry Commentary on the Whole Bible (Complete). Vol. 1, 1706. Bible Study Tools, www.biblestudytools.com/commentaries/matthew-henry-complete/.
[2] "Jewish Population by Country," Pew-Templeton Global Religious Futures Project, 2014. http://www.globalreligiousfutures.org/religions/jews.
[3] Carpenter, Eugene E, and Wayne McCown. Asbury Bible Commentary. Grand Rapids, Mich: Zondervan Pub. House, 1992. Print.
[4] 2 Corinthians 11:23-27.
[5] Zondervan KJV Commentary, Copyright 2010 by Zondervan. https://www.biblegateway.com/.
[6] Walvoord, John F., Zuck, Roy B., "Acts," In New Testament Edition of The Bible Knowledge Commentary, p.383. Colorado Springs: Victor Books, 1983.

WEEK 6

[1] Barker, Kenneth L, John R, Verlyn Verbrugge, and Richard Polcyn. 2004. *The Expositor's Bible Commentary*. Grand Rapids, Mich.: Zondervan.
[2] Warren, Rick. 2006. *The Purpose Driven Life*. Chagrin Falls, Oh: Zondervan.

[3] NIV Quest Study Bible. 2011. Grand Rapids, MI: Zondervan.
[4] Chester, Tim. 2011. A Meal with Jesus : Discovering Grace, Community, & Mission around the Table. Wheaton, Ill.: Crossway.
[5] The Definition of Hospitality." 2019. https://www.dictionary.com/browse/hospitality.
[6] What Exactly Is Biblical Hospitality?" n.d. Doctrine and Devotion. Accessed February 2, 2021. http://www.doctrineanddevotion.com/blog/what-exactly-is-biblical-hospitality.
[7] Tyree, Morgan. 2020. Your Hospitality Personality: How to Confidently Create Connection and Community.

Made in United States
Orlando, FL
10 September 2022

22262334R00076